CHINA AND SOCIALISM

CHINA AND SOCIALISM

Market Reforms and Class Struggle

MARTIN HART-LANDSBERG & PAUL BURKETT

MONTHLY REVIEW PRESS

New York

Library of Congress Cataloging-in-Publication Data

Hart-Landsberg, Martin.
    China and socialism : market reforms and class struggle / by Martin
    Hart-Landsberg and Paul Burkett.
        p. cm.
    Includes bibliographical references and index.
    ISBN 1-58367-123-4 (pbk.) — ISBN 1-58367-124-2 (cloth)
1. China—Economic policy—1976–2000. 2. China—Economic
conditions—1976–2000. 3. Socialism—China. I. Burkett, Paul,
1956 May 26– II. Title.
    HC427.92.H379 2005
    338.951—dc22

                                            2005000246

MONTHLY REVIEW PRESS
122 West 27th Street
New York, NY 10001
www.monthlyreview.org

Printed in Canada

10 9 8 7 6 5 4 3 2 1

Contents

FOREWORD by Harry Magdoff and John Bellamy Foster   7

PREFACE   13

INTRODUCTION: China and Socialism   15

1. China's Rise to Model Status   20

2. China's Economic Transformation   34

3. Contradictions of China's Transformation: Domestic   62

4. Contradictions of China's Transformation: International   87

5. China and Socialism: Conclusion   114

APPENDIX: Tables   121

NOTES   134

INDEX   152

Foreword

HARRY MAGDOFF and JOHN BELLAMY FOSTER

There is currently no lack of books on market reforms in China after Mao. However, the present study by Martin Hart-Landsberg and Paul Burkett is unique in that it is a well-grounded Marxist study of how a major post-revolutionary society turned away from socialism and toward the economics of capitalism. In addition, the current transformation in China throws light on why capitalism, by its very nature, creates poverty, inequality, and ecological destruction in the process of economic growth.

Socialism cannot be created overnight. A long transition is needed to build its political, human, and economic foundations. If we are to learn from the past, we need critical and ruthless analyses of the post-revolutionary societies, their achievements as well as failures. It should be evident by now that a transfer in class power can make a real difference. That shows up during the early days of a move to a new social system: elimination of hunger, creation of full employment, the spread of literacy, universal education and medical care for all the people, and an escape from imperialist domination. These steps toward social justice are not easy. Moreover, booby traps may slow and divert further progressive and radical changes.

The transition to full-fledged socialism entails a long and bumpy road full of pitfalls and contradictions. Time is needed to: (a) convert existing productive forces into worker-controlled and peasant-controlled enterprises, (b) create new productive forces for the basic needs of the entire population, and (c) construct a legal-political-cultural superstructure adapted to a cooperative commonwealth. Shortcuts are few and far between. Nor can general recipes be designed that will suit every country and anticipate every twist and turn of history. Room must be provided for a process of trial and error, which means informing and involving the masses, including the power of the masses to recall administrators and correct errors.

The socialist vision encompasses a nonhierarchical, egalitarian society—one which strives to improve the living standards and quality of life, with top priority given to the poorest, most discriminated against, and powerless. Thus, the dominant tendency in China during roughly the first 30 post-revolutionary years was to dedicate resources and effort to achieving equality and meeting the basic needs of the people, especially those of the downtrodden. By the end of the 1970s (covering roughly the first three decades after the revolutionists came to power), China had become a highly egalitarian society, arguably the most egalitarian on earth in terms of the distribution of income and in meeting basic needs. Since then, however, a striking turnaround has taken place—in fact as in theory. The heads of the party and the government encouraged a blossoming of private industry via domestic and foreign investment. A turn to so-called market socialism was proclaimed. The U-turn in the ruling ideology was dramatic. Market socialism, it was said, would lead to speedy growth of material production, a growth of riches that would inevitably trickle down to all social sectors.

China's new course has indeed resulted in an extremely rapid increase of production and total national income. However, the wealth created didn't trickle down very far. The result is a very rich upper stratum and a comfortable middle class, and as for the rest: poverty, insecurity, unemployment, and a decline in education and medical care. The effect of the turnaround is finally acknowledged in official circles. Last year the political department of China's Ministry of Finance issued a report on the subject. *People's Daily Online* (June 19, 2003) ran an article containing the substance of the document. The article began by acknowledging that the government report had revealed: (1) "A ceaseless widening of the gap in income distribution and the aggravated division of the rich and the poor is occurring"; and (2) "Amassed wealth is becoming more concentrated, with the difference of family fortunes becoming bigger and bigger."

What is clear from the Chinese experience is that the basis of the class struggle continues even after nationalization of business institutions. The mentality (ideology) of the old society does not evaporate into thin air after a revolutionary change. It remains and conflicts with the socialist road. Other strains arise from the potential and actual entrenchment of a bureaucratic elite, the persistence of hierarchy, and the complexity of building a people's democracy. The bureaucratic elite and other privileged groups sustain a competing ideology—one that justifies their privileges, which are at odds with the needs of the mass of the people. Members of the elite are commonly concerned with passing on their advantages to their children, typical of class society. The clash of class interests continues from generation to generation. In this way the class struggle persists, though in different forms from the past. At heart, as Mao pointed out, even some in high Communist Party positions wanted to take the "capitalist road."

The ideological struggle that takes place is linked with differences over the rate and direction of growth. Unfortunately, growth in itself is the deity worshipped by "capitalist roaders," whereas the crucial questions are: What kind of growth? For what purpose? For whose benefit? Should the growth be geared to satisfying the desires of intellectuals, managers, business owners, and the bureaucratic political groups and classes? Or, should the direction of growth be oriented towards improving living standards and quality of life for the mass of the people?

We can't discuss these questions in this space as fully as they should be. But some aspects need to be mentioned. Growth may be badly needed: houses for the homeless, medical centers, three meals a day for everyone, sewage and running water in the slums and ghettos, and so on. However, too speedy growth may be harmful to people and the environment. These are basic questions that distinguish between capitalism and socialism. Under capitalism, driven by profit for the few, accumulation occurs on a world scale while the great majority of the world's masses are plunged into misery. And as shown by Hart-Landsberg and Burkett, the Chinese case is witness to the fact that growth with the purpose of increasing profits, or growth merely for the sake of growth, leads inevitably to stark social inequality.

The work of Hart-Landsberg and Burkett is also significant in that it boldly confronts a fad in left-wing circles: a faith in "market socialism" as the proper and effective way to replace capitalism. Economic planning, it is claimed, has proven to be a failure: it just can't work. The issue is seen as a matter of technique—finding the right mechanism (plan or market), rather than a question of class or of meeting the most pressing human needs. Technocrats are supposed to have the answers—in this case a reliance on the magic of the market. But look at the Chinese success story! The theorists' enthusiasm for market socialism is small beer compared with the excitement that today's Chinese market has generated. Conventional pundits and corporate CEOs, who in their greed see only the fabulous riches being created and there for the taking, are blind to the real conditions of the people. CEOs are enthralled by the profit opportunities: on the one hand, an exceptionally large low-wage industrial reserve army, and on the other hand, untold millions of potential customers. Left and right revel in the exceptional, ongoing rates of economic growth. Nowhere is the enormous and continuing human cost of this distorted system of growth considered.

The issue can be approached in a simplified fashion. A national economy has two parts, consumption and investment. If more is spent on investment, less will be available for consumption. Economic growth depends on an increase in investment, aided by increases in labor productivity. But an increase in investment, especially when extremely rapid, will slow any increase in consumption by the masses. Although consumption as a whole may increase, consumption of the wealthy inevitably occurs at the expense of the poor when there are big differences in power and wealth. To the extent that a section of the population is able to spend much more than others, investment as well as production will concentrate on luxury goods and facilities for the wealthy. The Chinese government report referred to above (summarized in *People's Daily Online*) acknowledges that the gulf between the classes is increasing with the unusually fast growth: "A ceaseless widening of the gap in income distribution and the aggravated division of the rich and the poor is occurring."

The growing polarization in income and wealth and the slower increases (if any for the lower strata) in consumption among the masses are not the only negative consequences of ultra-fast growth. The shift to so-called market socialism followed the path dictated by capitalist globalization. According to the *Financial Times*, (May 4, 2004) "China [is set] to join the league of biggest direct investors abroad." Vice Premier Wu Yi, "in a written statement to the ongoing forum on 'going global' of Chinese enterprises [sponsored by the Ministry of Commerce] said this strategy will benefit not only China's development but also the prosperity of the whole world" (reported in the *People's Daily Online*, May 26, 2004). Moreover, the same source reports that China is promoting its transnationals: "China will further promote the 'going global' strategy and nurture more transnational companies, senior officials said." Government authorized foreign investment by Chinese firms was over $2 billion in 2003 and is expected to grow rapidly.

Another consequence of worshipping at the idol of rapid growth is the resulting ecological havoc. As the deputy director of China's State Environmental Administration, Pan Yue, has put it, "If we continue on this path of traditional industrial civilisation, then there is no chance that we will have sustainable development...[b]ecause China's populace, resources, environment has already reached the limits of its capacity to cope" (*New York Times*, May 24, 2004). The dammed Yangtze River has become a cesspool of sewage, poisoned because of nonexistent or inadequate treatment of industrial and human wastes. And according to Elizabeth Economy, senior fellow and director for Asia studies at the Council on Foreign Relations,

> There has been a dramatic increase in the demand for natural resources of all kinds, including water, land, and energy. Forest resources have been depleted, triggering a range of devastating secondary impacts, such as desertification, flooding, and species loss. At the same time, levels of water and air pollution have skyrocketed...More than 75% of the water in rivers flowing

through China's urban areas is unsuitable for drinking or fishing. Sixty million people have difficulty getting access to water, and almost three times that
number drink contaminated water daily. Desertification, which affects one-
quarter of China's land, is forcing tens of thousands of people to migrate
every year....(www.fas.harvard.edu/ffiasiactr/haq/200301/0301a001.htm)

China has seven of the ten cities with the most air pollution in the
world, and has 300 cities that fail to meet acceptable levels for total
suspended particulates as defined by the World Health Organization.

To summarize our argument—once a post-revolutionary country
starts down the path of capitalist development, especially when trying
to attain very rapid growth—one step leads to another until all the
harmful and destructive characteristics of the capitalist system finally
reemerge. Rather than promising a new world of "market socialism,"
what distinguishes China today is the speed with which it has erased
past egalitarian achievements and created gross inequalities and
human and ecological destruction. In our view, the present book by
Martin Hart-Landsberg and Paul Burkett deserves careful study as a
work that strips away the myth that Chinese socialism survives in the
midst of some of the most unrestrained capitalist practices. There is
no market road to socialism if that means setting aside the most
pressing human needs and the promise of human equality.

PREFACE

The Chinese economic experience remains the source of important lessons about the challenges of building socialism. However, the current lessons are mostly negative. Tragically, the Chinese government's program of "market reforms," which was allegedly supposed to reinvigorate socialism, has instead led the country down a slippery slope toward an increasingly capitalist, foreign-dominated development path. The resulting domestic and international social costs have been enormous. Compounding the tragedy is the fact that many progressives, including many who continue to support socialism, remain defenders of Chinese economic policies and encourage those in other countries to adopt similar policies.

We believe that this situation reflects a profound popular confusion about capitalist dynamics and socialism that must be overcome if we are to make meaningful progress toward building a better world. We sincerely hope that this study of China's "market socialist" experience will make a small but meaningful contribution to that outcome.

Many people contributed to our understanding of the Chinese experience, including its ideological and economic significance in the world today. In particular we would like to acknowledge Mike Lebowitz, Barbara Foley, Leo Panitch, Sam Ginden, Patrick Bond, Minqi Li, Andong Zhu, David Kotz, Victor Wallis, Susan Williams,

Stephen Frost, and Tim Pringle. We would also like to thank the editors of the *Korean Journal of Political Economy* for publishing an article by us that contained an earlier version of some of the book's ideas; Aimin Chen for providing access to her copies of the *China Statistical Yearbook*; Andrew Nash and the entire Monthly Review Press staff for their help and encouragement; and our families for their ongoing support—Sylvia Hart-Landsberg, Leah Hart-Landsberg, and Rose Hart-Landsberg, and Suzanne Carter along with Patrick Burkett and Molly Burkett. Finally, we wish to acknowledge our debt to the working people of China, not only for their past efforts at social change, but also for their ongoing struggles against "socialist capitalism" and for a real socialism.

INTRODUCTION

China and Socialism

China and socialism...during the three decades following the 1949 establishment of the People's Republic of China (PRC), it seemed as if these words would forever be joined in an inspiring unity. China had been forced to suffer the humiliation of defeat in the 1840–42 Opium War with Great Britain and the ever-expanding treaty port system that followed it. The Chinese people suffered under not only despotic rule by their emperor and then a series of warlords, but also under the crushing weight of imperialism, which divided the country into foreign-controlled spheres of influence. Gradually, beginning in the 1920s, the Chinese Communist Party led by Mao Zedong organized growing popular resistance to the foreign domination and exploitation of the country and the dictatorship of Chiang Kai-shek. The triumph of the revolution under the leadership of the Chinese Communist Party finally came in 1949, when the party proclaimed it would bring not only an end to the suffering of the people but a new democratic future based on the construction of socialism.

There can be no doubt that the Chinese revolution was a world historic event and that tremendous achievements were made under the banner of socialism in the decades that followed. However, it is our opinion that this reality should not blind us to three important facts: first, at the time of Mao's death in 1976, the Chinese people remained far from achieving the promises of socialism. Second, beginning in

1978 the Chinese Communist Party embarked on a market-based reform process that, while allegedly designed to reinvigorate the effort to build socialism, has actually led in the opposite direction and at great cost to the Chinese people. And finally, progressives throughout the world continue to identify with and take inspiration from developments in China, seeing the country's rapid export-led growth as either confirmation of the virtues of market socialism or proof that, regardless of labels, active state direction of the economy can produce successful development within a capitalist world system.

As much as we were also inspired by the Chinese revolution, we have for some time believed that this continuing identification by progressives with China and its "socialist market economy" represents not only a serious misreading of the Chinese reform experience but, even more important, a major impediment to the development of the theoretical and practical understandings required to actually advance socialism in China and elsewhere.

As we will argue in this book, it is our position that China's market reforms have led not to socialist renewal but rather to full-fledged capitalist restoration, including growing foreign economic domination. Significantly, this outcome was driven by more than simple greed and class interest. Once the path of pro-market reforms was embarked upon, each subsequent step in the reform process was largely driven by tensions and contradictions generated by the reforms themselves. The weakening of central planning led to ever more reliance on market and profit incentives, which in turn encouraged the privileging of private enterprises over state enterprises and, increasingly, of foreign enterprises and markets over domestic ones. Although a correct understanding of the dynamics of China's reform process supports the Marxist position that market socialism is an unstable formation, this important insight has largely been lost because of the continuing widespread belief by many progressives that China remains in some sense a socialist country. This situation cannot help but generate confusion about the meaning of socialism while strengthening the ideological position of those who oppose it.

Many other progressive scholars and activists dismiss arguments about the meaning of socialism as irrelevant to the challenges of development faced by people throughout the world. They look at China's record of rapid and sustained export-led growth and conclude that China is a development model, with a growth strategy that can and should be emulated by other countries. We believe, and argue in this book, that this celebration of China is a serious mistake, one that reflects a misunderstanding not only of the Chinese experience but also of the dynamics and contradictions of capitalism as an international system. In fact, an examination of the effects of China's economic transformation on the region's other economies makes clear that the country's growth is intensifying competitive pressures and crisis tendencies to the detriment of workers throughout the region, including in China.

Our differences with leftists and progressives might never have produced a book about China if it were not for our May 2003 trip to Cuba to attend an international conference on Marxism.[1] While in the country we sought to learn what we could about how Cuba was responding to its economic difficulties, and how the government's understanding of and commitment to socialism was shaping that response. We were told repeatedly that many Cuban economists looked to the Chinese "market socialist" growth strategy as an attractive model for Cuba.

We hoped that this was not true. But at the conference itself, when the discussion turned toward the challenges facing Cuba, several Cuban economists publicly endorsed the Chinese experience of rapid export-led growth based on foreign direct investment (FDI) as offering the only hope for Cuba to sustain its socialist project under current international conditions. Although these economists were only repeating arguments we had heard from progressives in other countries, they were especially jarring to hear at a conference concerned with the contemporary relevance of Marxism and in a context where there was little gain to be imagined for the economists making them. Fidel Castro was also at the conference and the Cuban government had already firmly rejected market socialism.

We are certainly not the first social scientists to criticize developments in China from a Marxist perspective.[2] But it seems clear to us that the importance of China in shaping debates about development and socialism has only grown. And we feel that the confusion surrounding China's post-reform experiences signifies a deeper theoretical and political confusion about Marxism and socialism that greatly hurts our collective efforts to build a world free from alienation, oppression, and exploitation. Thus, we have ventured to offer our own contribution to the study of China and socialism, focusing our critique on the economic dynamics, social consequences, and political implications of China's market reform process. Despite the fact that our work focuses on China, we hope and intend that the issues raised and considered will also have significance for people concerned with social developments and struggles in countries other than China.

Our book begins, in chapter 1, with a discussion of the rise of China as a positive reference point for development economists, with explanatory emphasis on the collapse of the Soviet Union and its satellite economies, the 1997–98 Asian crisis, and the tendency of both mainstream and left economists to formulate and rationalize their national policy visions by appealing to the apparently successful development experiences of individual "poster countries" rather than to the uneven development of accumulation and class conflict on a world scale.

In chapter 2, we critically examine the basic dynamics of China's market socialist reform process, showing how each step in China's transition—from planning to market, from domestic- to export-oriented production, and from state to private and increasingly foreign control—moved the system further away from any meaningful progress toward socialism in the sense of a system centered on grassroots worker-community needs and capabilities. This examination also makes clear that each step was a logical outcome not of any objective requirements for further development of human, natural, and social productive forces, but of the contradictions generated by previous reforms. We further show that the rapid economic growth that accompanied the reforms was largely due to factors other than efficiency gains from marketization and privatization. The arguments in this chapter undercut the widespread image of wise Chinese policymakers carefully and deliberately engineering a relatively stable, low-cost transition to a more productive market-driven regime.

In chapter 3, we focus on the main domestic contradictions of China's reform process. We show that the considerable costs of the pro-market transition (rising unemployment, economic insecurity, inequality, intensified exploitation, declining health and education conditions, exploding government debt, and unstable prices) are not transitional side effects but rather basic preconditions of economic growth cum rapid capital accumulation under Chinese conditions. We also highlight the growing (though somewhat fragmented) struggles of Chinese workers to defend the rights purportedly guaranteed to them by the pre-reform regime, and to protect themselves from some of the worst forms of exploitation under the new system in the face of ongoing government repression of all independent worker and community organizing.

In chapter 4, we argue that China's economic experience cannot be fully understood in isolation from the broader dynamics of global capitalism, especially uneven development and overproduction. In exploring these dynamics we highlight how China's economic transformation has benefited from as well as intensified the contradictions of capitalist development in other countries, especially East Asia. This perspective makes clear that China's foreign investment driven, export-led growth cannot be treated as simply a positive sum experience replicable by other nations.

We conclude by first summarizing the main lessons of our work, highlighting the continuing relevance of Marxist theory and the importance of building movements for change based on principles of international solidarity and through engagement with worker-community struggles against capitalist imperatives. Then we outline an alternative, worker-community centered approach to socialist development that treats exports and foreign investment as vehicles of grassroots needs and capabilities and of international solidarity.

I

China's Rise to Model Status

China's post-reform rapid economic rise has led many progressives to view the country as a development model whose experience proves that there are viable alternative paths to growth within the existing capitalist world system. Significantly, although not widely acknowledged by most of these progressives, many mainstream economists have also embraced China as a development model.

The basic facts that have anchored this celebration of the Chinese growth experience are well known. These are the country's high-speed economic expansion, fast-rising exports, and growing inflows of FDI. Tables 1 and 2 provide some indicators of these trends.* According to the official data, China not only enjoyed double-digit real GDP growth for most of the decade 1985–95, but also maintained rapid growth of over 7 percent per year during and after the 1997–98 East Asian crisis. That exports played a major role in this expansion is clear from their high growth rates and their increasing ratio to GDP. United Nation Conference on Trade and Development (UNCTAD) figures show that as of 2000, China had the fourth-largest share of world exports, 6.1 percent, trailing only the United States, Germany, and Japan. Its increase in export share over the period 1985–2000 was the greatest of any country, more than twice that of the second-place United States.[1]

Annual net FDI inflows into China also exploded in value, growing from only US$1 billion in 1985 to over US$50 billion by 2002, with FDI accounting for a significant share of the country's capital investment during this period. "Even in 2001 and 2002, when global flows of foreign direct investment fell by about a half and a third, respectively, inflows into China continued to expand"; so much so that in the latter year China became "the world's number-one destination for foreign direct investment."[2]

However, these are just facts. They do not explain why they have become the basis for a shared celebration of China as the model developing country by development economists across the political spectrum. While the rest of this book is dedicated to a critique of this view of the Chinese experience, it is important that we first explore the changing global-historical context that produced it. Doing so helps to clarify some of the theoretical and political confusions as well as challenges that must be overcome if we are to advance the socialist project.

CHINA AS A NEOLIBERAL MODEL

The post-1989 breakup of the Soviet Union, and adoption of neoliberal policies by the ex-Soviet republics and former Soviet-satellite countries of Eastern Europe, at first created an unabashedly triumphant atmosphere in neoliberal circles. The rapid moves by erstwhile "socialist" governments to end planning, privatize state enterprises, and open up markets to imports and foreign investment, all with advice and support from the International Monetary Fund (IMF) and World Bank, seemed to validate neoliberal "end of history" thinking. Tragically, these "shock therapy" policies led to major economic collapses (especially in Russia) with devastating consequences for East European working people that continue to this day. These setbacks had two effects on mainstream development thinking.

First, they instigated a debate over the proper pace and sequencing, and institutional requirements, of neoliberal reforms.[3] While conservative neoliberals like Jeffrey Sachs tended to blame the disastrous results of shock therapy on government corruption and lack of credible commitment to reforms, left-wing neoliberals like Joseph Stiglitz questioned the wisdom of immediate wholesale liberalization and privatization. The latter group recommended more deliberate reform programs in which macroeconomic stability and confidence would take precedence over the abrupt freeing of trade and short-term capital flows.

However, despite these differences, both groups of neoliberals remained committed to the ultimate goals of a competitive market economy, free trade, and free capital movements. Accordingly, both saw export competitiveness and attraction of FDI as key components of successful development. In this sense, mainstream development debates in the wake of the shock therapy disasters actually clarified the core elements of the neoliberal consensus.

Second, given the continued dominance of the notion that "there is no alternative" (TINA) to neoliberal capitalism, the post-Soviet collapses encouraged the search for new neoliberal success stories that could be held up as examples for other countries to follow. The opportunism underlying this strategy was evident from past attempts to use South Korea as a free-market poster country even though it had clearly not followed free-market policies (gradual or otherwise) toward either trade or FDI. The problem was that there were no other obvious capitalist development successes available.[4] Hence, when, by the early 1990s, it became clear that Thailand, Malaysia, and Indonesia were experiencing rapid economic growth driven largely by FDI and manufactured exports, South Korea was quickly dropped as model country in favor of these emerging export platforms for transnational capital. Then came the East Asian crisis, which necessitated yet another search for new poster countries. That this search led to China reflects both the tactical disagreements and the fundamental consensus between conservative and left-wing neoliberals.[5]

The response by conservative neoliberals to the East Asian debt crisis was crassly opportunistic. They dismissed the crisis-affected countries—which literally weeks or even days before had been praised as free-market success stories—as hopelessly corrupt "crony capitalist" regimes in desperate need of wholesale free-market restructuring. The IMF and the crisis-affected governments followed this advice, implementing currency devaluations, monetary fiscal retrenchments, and disruptive privatization schemes in debt-ridden economies already in recession. They backed off somewhat only when it became clear that a replication of the post-Soviet shock therapy disaster was in progress (and that most plum East Asian enterprises had already been plucked by foreign investors).

Meanwhile, in order to defend the benefits of their policies, conservative neoliberals shifted their attention to Mexico, a country that in the early 1990s they had counseled to learn from East Asia, and whose earlier failures with neoliberal reforms had been blamed on corruption and cronyism. Still, Mexico sustained positive economic growth during the 1996–2000 period. Even more important, it did so while restructuring its economy as a manufactured export platform by liberalizing FDI and trade, suppressing workers' wage demands, and privatizing state-owned industrial enterprises and banks. Thus, Mexico became the new model country and was now favorably compared to East Asia.

Its newly acquired fame proved short-lived. Mexico fell into recession in 2001, in large measure because its neoliberal policies had greatly increased its dependence on exports to a U.S. economy that was now in recession. However, even when the United States experienced a weak recovery, Mexico continued to stagnate as more and more foreign export producers began shifting production to China where wages were considerably lower.[6] Conservative neoliberals responded first by scolding Mexico for its corruption and inadequate dedication to cost efficiency and free-market reforms. Then, they began citing China's spectacular economic record as proof of the power of neoliberalism, especially of "an unwavering commitment to reform."[7] If China succeeded where Mexico failed, said the World Bank, this was because the former more effectively "transformed itself from a hostile investment environment" by more decisively "embrac[ing] globalization in the areas of trade and foreign direct investment."[8]

Left-wing neoliberals had a different response to the East Asian crisis: they blamed it on the premature deregulation of domestic finance and (especially) short-term cross-border capital flows. Joseph Stiglitz and others also criticized the tight macro-policies (especially high interest rates), exchange-rate devaluations, and crash privatization and deregulation measures implemented by the IMF and East Asian governments. They argued that they would only deepen the region's recession, destabilize national and regional financial systems, and further weaken business confidence.

The left-wing neoliberals were right to criticize these policy responses, even though their analysis of the causes of the crisis itself was quite shallow—ignoring such crucial factors as intensified competition for FDI, the import intensity of FDI-based export production, regional and global overproduction, and endogeneity of capital-market liberalization with respect to these and other contradictions of export-led growth.[9] But, for present purposes, the important point about the left-wing neoliberal analysis of the crisis is that it also led to a favorable depiction of China, one that did not fundamentally deviate from the core tenet of neoliberalism, namely that "the spread of global capitalism has enormous potential to benefit the poor."[10]

Stiglitz thus pointed to China's regime of capital controls and its expansionary macro-policies to explain the country's insulation from the worst effects of the East Asian crisis.[11] Building on this comparison, he painted a broader picture of China "as an example of a country that has successfully integrated into the global marketplace—but in a manner that defies the conventional wisdom of the Washington Consensus."[12] According to this analysis, "China has adopted privatization and lowered trade barriers,...but in a gradual manner that has prevented the social fabric from being torn apart in the process. With little advice from the IMF, it has achieved high growth rates while reducing poverty."[13] Unlike the Russian experience with shock therapy, says Stiglitz,

China put creating competition, new enterprises and jobs, before privatization and restructuring existing enterprises. While China recognized the importance of macrostabilization, it never confused ends with means, and it never took fighting inflation to an extreme. It recognized that if it was to maintain social stability, it had to avoid massive unemployment. Job creation had to go in tandem with restructuring. When China liberalized, it did so gradually and in ways that ensured that resources that were displaced were redeployed to more efficient uses, not left in fruitless unemployment.[14]

Indeed, "speaking in Beijing in July 1998," Stiglitz "called China 'by far the most successful of the low-income countries' in moving to a market economy."[15]

This depiction of a smooth and low-cost marketization of the Chinese economy is a one-sided idealization. Nonetheless, it allowed Stiglitz and other left-wing neoliberals to stake out an autonomous short- and medium-term policy stance while still pledging allegiance to markets, free trade, and FDI—in short, insertion into the global-capitalist division of labor—as the only viable path to economic development. Nicholas Lardy provides a useful summary of this common neoliberal core as applied to China:

> China's growth prospects…remain strong. In large part, this is because of the cumulative effect of more than two decades of economic reform. Most importantly, the process of gradual price liberalization has proceeded so far that markets now set the prices of almost all commodities. Equally important, reforms have dramatically increased competition, not just in manufacturing but in construction and much of the service sector as well. The pervasiveness of market-determined prices and competitive markets has improved the efficiency of resource allocation….The role of the external sector in increasing competition in the domestic market is especially important, and all too frequently underestimated.[16]

Such is the image of China as, for the moment at least, the leading neoliberal poster country.

CHINA AS A PROGRESSIVE MODEL

The dismantling of the purportedly socialist economies of the Soviet Union and Eastern Europe put many leftists on the defensive. Naturally, left economists became interested in China, though for reasons that, on the surface at least, were diametrically opposed to neoliberalism. Quite different from the rapid ideological and structural transformations accompanying Russian-type "shock therapy," China's government continued to proclaim its commitment to building socialism. Moreover, its more gradualist reform policies were producing rapid and sustained economic growth.

The decentralizing and market-oriented nature of China's econom-ic reforms enhanced the country's attractiveness to many on the left, especially academics. Mainstream economists had long argued that central planning and state ownership were inefficient, and the rejection of socialism and embrace of capitalism by East European governments seemed to verify the correctness of this position. To many leftists, China's reform program at first seemed to offer a "third way" between capitalism and centralized state-socialism. While maintaining a core role for state enterprises, it reduced central planning of the economy, enhanced the authority of local governments, created new forms of enterprise organization (including small private as well as collective township and village enterprises), and promoted profit- and productiv-ity-based worker-compensation incentives as well as market relations to stimulate the efficiency of all enterprises, including those in the still dominant state sector. These "market socialist" policies appeared immune to the standard critique of central planning, and they were easier to defend using the discourse of mainstream market analysis in an increasingly neoliberal-dominated academic world.

By the early 1990s, a number of progressive and left academics were writing articles that, while cautious about the future, demon-strated a strong belief in the viability and even superiority of market socialism based in large part on China's strong economic perform-ance. M. J. Gordon, for example, argued that

> China's experience since 1978 has demonstrated that policies that may be characterized as "market socialism" provide a viable and successful alterna-tive....While these reforms may not be a model that should simply be dupli-cated elsewhere, they reveal that a middle way is feasible.[17]

Similarly, Victor Lippit used China's experience to question the notion that "the Cold War is over and capitalism appears to have won completely":

> China's economic success forces us to consider more carefully the popular thesis that consigns socialism to history. Public policy in China is directed toward establishing a system of market socialism, one in which state-owned

enterprises coexist with collectively and privately owned ones. If such a mix of modes of production can be maintained, and if popular/democratic control over the economic and political life of the nation can be established, it is quite possible that the present will prove to be a period of socialist transition. If, to the contrary, the capitalist enterprises overwhelm their state and collective counterparts, then capitalist transition will be the order of the day. The point is that the issue remains to be decided, and since the possibilities for socialist development remain, consideration of the Chinese case provides a new perspective for thinking about the alleged victory of capitalism.[18]

In sum, China's apparent success with market-socialist reforms not only gave many leftists renewed hope that neoliberal, globalized capitalism was not really the end of history; it also served as a positive reference point for reinterpreting the struggle between capitalism and socialism on a world scale.[19]

China's analytical and ideological resonance was not purely academic. Interest in the Chinese model was also strong in the few remaining state-socialist countries, especially Vietnam and Cuba. After all, with the collapse of the Soviet system, Cuba itself suffered a serious economic shock. It desperately needed a new strategy, one that could generate foreign exchange to make up for its loss of markets and foreign aid.

Cuban economists as well as the Cuban government were naturally impressed by China's sustained economic growth, and even more so by its increasingly successful efforts to attract FDI and generate manufactured exports. An initial period of study was followed in 1995 by a trip to China and Vietnam by Fidel Castro, and a draft proposal for restructuring Cuba's economic strategy that was strongly influenced by the Chinese experience.[20] Although the Cuban government subsequently announced that it would not pursue the socialist market strategies followed by China and Vietnam, Cuban economists have continued to admire China's successful "incorporation into global networks" of manufacturing production and trade, an incorporation that one Cuban economist has deemed "essential for development today."[21]

Indeed, many Cuban economists are still calling for a system of government actions to help Cuba attract more complex manufacturing processes tied to global production networks as a supplement to tourism and other current sources of foreign exchange.[22] Despite protestations to the contrary, this is clearly an argument for Cuba to adopt an export-oriented, foreign-driven growth strategy, which would require the enhanced use of market forces, the creation of a mixed economy, and decentralization of state enterprises—all of which appear to be strongly influenced by the Chinese model.

The reticence of the Cuban government to officially acknowledge China as a model is certainly understandable, given that China's reform process has worked to strengthen market forces and capitalist social relations at the expense of socialism.[23] More broadly, the number of leftists who viewed China as progressing on the road to socialism also declined over the decade of the 1990s as the outcome of the reforms became clearer. But this trend has not seriously challenged the position of the broader progressive community, which continues to see China as a positive model for development policy.

The resiliency of China-as-model thinking in the face of the country's evident capitalist restoration was made possible by the combination of China's export and growth successes with several historical-intellectual tendencies on the left. Among those still openly socialist in orientation, the recognition that China was moving away from socialism rarely generated an analysis of the significance of China's transformation for the uneven development and supersession of capitalism on a world scale, in the tradition, say, of classical Marxist analyses of the earlier rise of new national and regional centers of capitalist dynamism.[24]

Such large-scale, structural, and strategic-historical narratives were out of fashion in the "end of history" atmosphere that developed after 1989, especially with the rise of postmodernist thinking associated with the ongoing academicization of Western Marxism. It therefore appeared to many socialists that the best that could be hoped for in development theory and policy was a defensive struggle against neoliberalism and for political democracy rather than a frontal assault on capitalism. While this perspective did not always translate into full support for the Chinese model, it did tend to limit both systematic criticism of China's development strategy and the envisioning of non-capitalist alternatives.

Meanwhile, many other progressives had become thoroughly disillusioned with and estranged from official socialism and Marxism (both before and after the Soviet collapse). This group quite consciously had looked to East Asia to find models of socioeconomic organization that would help them oppose and build alternatives to neoliberalism. In the 1980s and early 1990s, Japan was the most popular model, with progressives pointing to its strong interventionist state, allegedly harmonious workplace relations, full employment, relative income equality, and superior export performance as evidence that its system was more worker-friendly and more efficient than neoliberal, U.S.-style capitalism. In this "progressive competitiveness" view, the Japanese experience showed that a socially oriented state and corporate system of capitalism could and should be pursued for both humane and economic reasons.[25]

By the mid-1990s, however, the Japanese economy was clearly in long-run stagnation. Advocates of progressive competitiveness gradually shifted their attention to South Korea and occasionally some of the new Southeast Asian export platforms, especially Thailand and Malaysia. Then came the crisis of 1997–98, and these countries floundered. Perhaps even more damaging to the progressive position was that the governments of these countries responded to their respective national crises by largely embracing the neoliberal explanation of the crisis and adopting neoliberal policies.

Forced to search for alternative models, and lacking both the (Marxist) analytical tools and the (class) politics needed to envision them from the standpoint of worker-community struggles in and against the uneven development of global capitalism, many progressives were naturally drawn to China. China was increasingly following a growth model similar to that followed by the former East Asian success stories but, in sharp contrast to those countries, had resisted abrupt liberalization and therefore weathered the regional crisis with minimal disruption.

In fact, the arguments progressives made to justify their admiration for the Chinese system were quite similar to those made by left-wing neoliberals, and this explains the growing popularity of Joseph Stiglitz's writings on the left. Like Stiglitz, progressives credited China's ongoing economic successes to its more controlled and limited liberalization of trade and finance. And like Stiglitz, they applauded China's reliance on FDI rather than unstable short-term capital inflows (which the Chinese government continued to tightly regulate). They both also agreed that China's resistance to currency devaluation was a critical policy decision that kept the East Asian crisis from being far worse than it was.

In this way, progressives tried to use left-wing neoliberal analysis to reassert some of their earlier progressive competitiveness arguments against neoliberalism. China was growing fast and had maintained at least a verbal commitment to a socialized (state and collective) sector and planning. Yet, it had also decentralized and increased market forces, even becoming one of the world's foremost exporters and attractors of productive FDI.

An array of progressive-left forces thus found themselves endorsing the Chinese experience, little troubled by whether it was socialist or not. Some scholars even extended their admiration of China's ongoing economic dynamism to expatriate Chinese business networks operating throughout the entire "Greater China" region.[26] In any event, the significance of China's revolutionary legacy was mostly reduced to its role in creating a strong state and other conditions for the country's current economic dynamism and competitiveness, as opposed to its potential for empowering working people and communities. Past achievements in the areas of wealth and income distribution and mass living standards were mentioned mainly to loosely connect them with China's successful insertion into the global capitalist economy. Walden Bello, for example, wrote that China's

> economic dynamism can't be separated from an event that most of us in the
> South missed out on: a social revolution in the late forties and early fifties
> that eliminated the worst inequalities in the distribution of land and income,
> and prepared the country for economic take-off when market reforms were
> introduced in the agricultural sector in the late 1970s....China likewise under-
> lines the critical contribution to future economic development of a liberation

movement that decisively wrests control of the national economy from foreign interests. China is a strong state, born in revolution and steeled in several decades of wars hot and cold....The difference is underlined by China's relationship with foreign capital compared with most countries in the South. Beijing is tough on foreign investors and has the upper hand in its relationship with the international business community. Yet foreign investors are scrambling to get into China, restrictions and all....Respect is what the Chinese government gets from investors. Respect is what our governments don't have. When it comes to pursuing national economic interests, what separates China from many of our countries is a successful revolutionary nationalist struggle that got institutionalized into a no-nonsense state.[27]

In this fashion, progressive competitiveness thinking converts socialism and revolution from instruments of human development and liberation into preconditions for capitalist development and competitiveness. Often overlooked by those who embrace this perspective is the fact that foreign investors' respect for the Chinese government, and their willingness to put up with "restrictive" terms on FDI, are largely due to the willingness of the Chinese government to deliver large supplies of cheap and productive labor power. Said differently, the facile linkage of China's post-revolutionary achievements to its current capitalist successes diverts attention from the main precondition of the latter: an increasingly insecure labor force whose efforts at self-organization are constantly suppressed by one of the world's most authoritarian states.

THE CONFUSION OVER CHINA

The embrace of China by both progressives and neoliberals demonstrates the analytical and ideological confusion that exists in the post–Cold War era. Unfortunately, the process of lurching from one poster country to another in response to capitalism's contradictions tends to be much more harmful to the left than to mainstream analysts and policy makers. The most general reason is that neoliberal political forces operate from a position of power and can dominate the interpretation of events and thus ideological conflicts.

A more specific reason is that the sequential search for national models tends to encourage the presumption that one can build progressive policy programs based on the capitalist growth experiences of individual nations. The problem—as Marx, Lenin, and Trotsky recognized—is that national success stories cannot be understood in isolation from the broader dynamics and contradictions of capitalism on regional and global levels. Given capitalism's uneven development and crises, national model–type thinking quickly leads to an endless pursuit of one success story after another, each more problematic than the last. The end result is that we lose any sense of alternative vision, theoretical clarity, and grassroots political resonance.

The foregoing sketch of China's rise to model status has focused on broad tendencies within neoliberalism and the progressive community. In reality, of course, there is not a complete consensus on China on either the left or the right. Here again, however, the presence of unqualified disagreements tends to be more crippling for progressives than for neoliberals.

Although neoliberals often disagree on the exact amount of progress a country has made along the path of free-market reforms (for some, no amount of deregulation and privatization is ever sufficient), their disagreements give neoliberalism a significant amount of wiggle room should its current poster country or countries suffer unexpected crises. Despite China's current model status, it is not hard to find neoliberal warnings about possible future setbacks if the reform process is not completed and corruption not weeded out. In the meantime, neoliberals use China's reform experience to criticize Cuba for not more fully marketizing its economy.[28] If things go bad in China another free-market success story can always be found to favorably contrast with Cuba and other "backward" nations.

For those interested in radical change toward a worker-community-centered economy, however, analytical disagreements are likely to involve different perceptions of collective values, vision, and strategy, i.e., matters that are not simply reversible without great political costs. After all, for progressives, movement building anchored by clear and consistent values, vision, and strategy is a necessity, whereas quite the opposite is true for defenders of the status quo. For the defenders, mass political demobilization is a positive value and the confusion generated by the rapid replacement of one model of success with another only encourages that demobilization.

In sum, not only do we disagree with those progressives who view China as a development model (whether socialist or not), we think the process by which they arrived at this position highlights an even more serious problem: the progressive community's general rejection of Marxism, which is—we believe—the most effective framework for understanding capitalism as well as building movements capable of superseding it. Thus, this engagement with China represents far more than an academic debate over the experiences of one country; it is about developing the theoretical clarity and strategic perspective necessary to help us transform the world.

2

China's Economic Transformation

When the leaders of China's Communist Party announced their program of market socialist reforms in 1978, they argued that it was necessary to overcome the country's growing problems of economic stagnation and waste caused by the Mao era's overly centralized state systems of planning and production. Rapid growth and industrial transformation during the 1980s encouraged many on the left, both inside and outside of China, to view market socialism as an attractive vehicle for achieving sustained growth, an egalitarian distribution of goods and services, and democratic participation in economic decision making.

However, despite the hopes of many on the left, it is our argument that China's market reform process has led the country not toward a new form of socialism, but rather an increasingly hierarchical and brutal form of capitalism. In this chapter we seek to answer the question of how and why, in less than two decades, a reform process that was seen as capable of promoting socialist renewal could end up leading to capitalist restoration.

The easy answer to this question is that the process was hijacked by party elites who feared losing their privileges. Faced with popular demands for change, they sought a reform process that would enable them to achieve a more secure form of control over the wealth of the country, and that led them, through trial and error, to embrace capitalism with "Chinese characteristics."

While there can be little doubt that the party elite has indeed profited from the ongoing process of capitalist restoration, we believe that this outcome was driven by more than simple greed. As we argue below, the capitalist restoration in China was also the result of structural contradictions generated by the reform process itself. While every country's experience is shaped by specific historical factors, and thus unique, we believe that this understanding of the Chinese experience offers important lessons for socialists everywhere. More specifically, we believe that the Chinese experience represents a strong argument against the viability of market socialism as a stable and progressive form of workers' empowerment.

HISTORICAL CONTEXT FOR POST-MAO ECONOMIC REFORMS

China under Mao followed a strategy for building socialism that emphasized heavy industry, centralized economic planning, state ownership of the means of production, and party control over political and cultural life. The Chinese revolution and resulting state policies succeeded in ending foreign domination of the country and feudal relations in the countryside and achieving full employment, basic social security, and generalized equality for Chinese working people.[1]

However, these broad and significant achievements came at great social cost. The upheavals associated with the Great Leap Forward (1958–61) and the Cultural Revolution (1966–76) involved considerable social instability and loss of life. Urban workers also became increasingly frustrated by the party's resistance to industrial democracy, including its opposition to a greater role for workers in enterprise management. The sole legal union federation, the All-China Federation of Trade Unions, proved no help. Operating under tight party control, its main responsibility was to promote production and labor discipline.[2] Strikes for higher wages and greater worker self-organization and independence took place in 1949–52, 1956–57, and 1966–67.[3] Jackie Sheehan gives some sense of the organizational efforts and political orientation underlying and growing out of these actions:

By the late spring of 1957, the high point of both the Hundred Flowers campaign and the wave of industrial unrest which had built up through the previous year, party authorities were...facing not just individual discontent, but organized collective resistance from some parts of the workforce. Autonomous unions were formed, often termed "redress grievance societies," and while many of these groups were confined to a single enterprise, there was also some liaison and coordination of action between enterprises and districts....Workers themselves knew that the difficulties they were experiencing were by and large a direct result of national decisions on individual and managements policy, now that everything from wage rates to lengths of apprenticeships had been standardized across all industries and regions, and accordingly "much of their wrath was directed against cadres in factory, government, Party and union positions."[4]

Increasing popular dissatisfaction with economic, political, and social trends finally led to the Tiananmen incident of April 5, 1976. The day before, a traditional day for honoring the dead, up to half a million Chinese had laid wreaths and poems at Tiananmen Square in memory of Zhou Enlai (who had died the previous January). Because Zhou had been criticized during the Cultural Revolution by the Red Guards (in part for defending some of its victims), the Chinese government interpreted this act as a criticism of its policies. It "removed the wreaths from the Square overnight, which led to violent and widespread unrest the day after, April Fifth. The resulting movement was dominated by workers and organized around the workplace. The government's crackdown was correspondingly brutal as workers voiced dissenting opinions on the widespread existence of favoritism, hypocrisy and inequality."[5]

Thus, despite the very real achievements of the revolution, the Chinese people at the time of Mao's death in September 1976 still remained far from enjoying steady and secure increases in their standard of living or exercising democratic control over their economic and political life. Mao's death therefore provided an important opportunity for the Chinese people to reevaluate past efforts, shape new initiatives, and advance the building of socialism in China.

Deng Xiaoping, who had been criticized by Mao during the Cultural Revolution for being a "capitalist roader," proved a wily political strategist. He was able to take advantage of the uncertainties of the immediate post-Mao period to quickly rehabilitate himself on the basis of his call for "unity and stability."[6] In late 1978, he succeeded Mao to become China's paramount leader.

Publicly proclaiming his commitment to socialism, Deng pursued the creation of what he and his allies called market socialism. Their position was that Mao had left the country in a dismal economic situation, largely because his policies had been too ideological and not in keeping with a scientific understanding of objective conditions. They argued that the critical task of the party was to help build the country's forces of production, which would require the introduction of market forces. Only market forces could overcome China's existing stagnation and ensure the economic progress needed to advance the process of building socialist relations of production.[7]

In reality, the Chinese economy at the end of the 1970s was far from a disaster, especially in industry. For example, between 1952 and the end of the Mao era, industrial output increased at an average annual rate of 11.2 percent. Despite disruptions to production during the Cultural Revolution decade (1966–76), industrial production still grew at an annual average rate of over 10 percent.[8] Moreover, these gains were achieved with little outside assistance. In fact, with the exception of Soviet aid during the 1950s, China faced a hostile economic environment. As a result, China was one of the few third world countries to enter the decade of the 1980s with no foreign debt.

Agricultural development was, on balance, far less successful. For example, food production barely matched the growth in population. As Maurice Meisner explains:

> Rural living standards were virtually stagnant over the final two decades of the Mao era, rising on average by less than 1 percent per annum, and that from a miserably low base. Whereas the gross value of industrial output increased tenfold from 1952 to 1975, agricultural output grew only twofold. Even that gain was attained only by vastly increasing the size of the agricultural workforce.[9]

Among the reasons for this poor record were inadequate investment in agriculture, the maintenance of adverse terms of trade for farm products in order to subsidize heavy industry, and the generally authoritarian and inflexible character of agricultural management under the commune system.[10] At the same time, Chinese peasants did enjoy meaningful improvements in public health, housing, education, and social security through the commune system. Moreover, "the extreme polarization of wealth that existed before 1949 was gone."[11] Even in terms of production itself, China's agricultural sector was still outperforming those of many other third world countries. As Mark Selden noted, "In 1977 China grew 30 to 40 percent more food per capita [than India] on 14 percent less arable land and distributed it far more equitably to a population which is 50 percent larger."[12]

Nonetheless, at the close of the Mao era, China's economy faced growing problems that could only be overcome through the adoption of new state policies. Economic planning had become overly centralized and, as the economy grew more complex, unable to effectively and efficiently respond to people's needs. There was overproduction of some goods and underproduction of others, inefficient transportation and distribution, and difficulties with poor product quality.

There were also problems in the organization of industrial production, where productivity was declining and output increases were sustained largely through ever-larger capital investments and a growing industrial labor force. Factories employed workers under conditions of lifetime employment, which meant that in many cases workers were being employed in unproductive activities. Wages were set nationally and basically frozen at their 1956 level. In addition, workers were given little opportunity or encouragement to take control over the conditions of production and reshape them as necessary.

The economy also suffered from investment imbalances, with too many resources being channeled into heavy industry at the expense of light industry and agriculture. The peasantry paid for this strategy with low prices for, and compulsory transfers to the state of, their output. Industrial workers suffered from a lack of consumer goods.

The Cultural Revolution, which was an attempt to shake up the system, also had negative consequences that went beyond the disruption of production, investment, and technological development. Rather than empowering working people by strengthening their collective organization, it wore them out with constant campaigns orchestrated from above, leaving them less motivated by social or moral appeals. And it was followed by a reassertion of hierarchical party control both in production and at all levels of society.[13] For example, unions were basically suspended during the Cultural Revolution. When they were finally reactivated in the late 1970s, they were reorganized to ensure greater party control over their activities.[14]

In short, the system was grinding down, and worker and peasant dissatisfaction was growing. There was a critical need to build on the strengths of China's past achievements while empowering workers and peasants to create new structures of decision making and planning. Among other things, this implied a restructuring and decentralization of the economy and state decision making to enhance the direct control of the associated producers over the conditions and products of their labor. Unfortunately this is not the way that the post-Mao government responded to the people's desire for change.

THE POST-MAO REFORM PROCESS

The party, led by Deng, argued that solving China's economic problems required raising the country's productive forces and not further experimentation with new socialist relations of production. And, according to Deng, the best way to enhance these productive forces was through greater use of markets. Markets would help overcome past problems of centralized decision making and allow for more efficient use of productive resources, including labor. The predicted result would be more rapid growth and technological progress, as well as sustained increases in consumption and consumer well-being.

It was the party's decision to marketize the Chinese economy. There were no mass movements seeking to solve China's many economic and social problems by strengthening market forces. As Robert Weil explains:

> "Markets" were imposed on the Chinese people by government fiat, notably
> in the forcible breaking up of the agricultural commune system which had
> been developed under the leadership of Mao Zedong, to be replaced with a

system of individual family contracts, and in the equally rapid and forcible demolition of socialist forms of collective public welfare now being imposed on state-owned enterprises and all the other major institutional centers of the society, including universities.[15]

As we shall see, while it may have been a party decision to begin marketization, market imperatives quickly proved uncontrollable. Each stage in the reform process generated new tensions and contradictions that were resolved only through a further expansion of market power, leading to the growing consolidation of a capitalist political economy. Thus, rather than "using capitalism to build socialism" as reformers argued would be the case, the reality has been that market socialism "used socialism to build capitalism."[16]

THE REFORM PROCESS: STAGE I (1978–83)

The greater use of market forces was presented, at the Third Plenum of the Chinese Communist Party in December 1978, as the key to achieving a "historic shift to socialist modernization." The party called for giving more authority to regional and provincial planning bodies, giving greater power to state firm managers to organize production, and encouraging more diverse forms of production, including cooperative and private firms. According to party pronouncements, centralized planning would still shape the overall structure and direction of economic activity but new growth would now increasingly be promoted and organized by the actions of these newly strengthened economic actors. The key element underpinning and giving coherence to this new approach was to be the creative and flexible use of markets. State firms and local governmental bodies would be motivated by a new freedom to pursue profits, and market forces would ensure that their individual decisions would be responsive to both people's needs and the overall planning initiatives of the party.

The reforms were first introduced in selected urban areas in early 1979. Central to the state's efforts to promote market socialism was the creation of a labor market. Without the freedom to freely allocate "labor resources," managers would be unable to rationally restructure production in response to market signals and thereby increase the overall efficiency and productivity of the economy. Because the government recognized that this policy undermined an important achievement of the Chinese revolution, it began by pursuing labor market reforms through pilot programs in which managers at selected enterprises were given the power to terminate lifetime employment contracts, discipline workers, and even close some inefficient firms.

In 1983, the state took a major step by ordering state enterprises to hire new workers on a contractual basis, meaning that their employment would be for a limited time, with none of the job security and welfare benefits enjoyed by regular state workers.[17] "By April 1987 China's state-owned enterprises (SOEs) had enrolled 7.51 million contract workers, about 8 percent of the industrial workforce," and an additional 6 million state-enterprise workers faced "employment reforms, which would result in their becoming contract employees."[18] One obvious effect of the contract labor system was to increase inequalities and divisions within the industrial working class.

Selected state firms were also allowed to produce and sell goods above regulated government prices after meeting plan targets. In addition, the larger state enterprises were allowed to retain a share of their profits for investment and bonuses.[19]

The private sector also received new encouragement as part of the reform process. Initially, private enterprises were restricted to employing fewer than seven family members and "apprentices." However, that limit was rarely enforced; it was abolished altogether in 1987. The private sector workforce grew from about 240,000 at the end of the 1970s, to 1.1 million in 1981, and 3.4 million in 1984.[20]

The state simultaneously encouraged the growth of urban collective enterprises. These included some sizable industrial operations producing light consumer goods, smaller industrial enterprises producing more traditional handicrafts, and relatively large retail and service companies. Although initially dependent on the state sector, the urban collectives were "profit-oriented...and many of them are in fact private firms wearing a fake 'red cap' for supplies, credit, and tax expediency."[21] Collective workers were fully wage workers, rather than collective owners of their enterprises. Moreover, they enjoyed none of the job protections or benefits of state workers and were also commonly paid less than state workers. Table 3 shows that by the mid-1980s, urban collectives accounted for significant shares of total employment in the manufacturing and domestic trade sectors.

Despite these initiatives, state enterprises remained dominant and state planning directed most economic activity during this first stage. For example, as of the mid-1980s, state enterprises still employed approximately 70 percent of all urban workers. Nonetheless, as indicated in table 3, this represented a significant decline from their 78 percent share of urban employment in 1978. The relative decline in employment in state enterprises was especially pronounced in the domestic trade sector.

Significantly, even at the very beginning of the reform process, the state placed great importance on attracting foreign multinational corporations. One of the reasons was that foreign firms were considered the best vehicle for introducing and legitimizing the capitalist-oriented market principles that the party hoped to encourage. The party could not hope to immediately convert state enterprises into profit-maximizing firms. Managers and workers had little experience with market processes and many could be expected to oppose them for a variety of reasons. Foreign firms, on the other hand, expected and could be granted substantial freedom over the organization and direction of their economic activity and could therefore serve to model and encourage the desired domestic restructuring of production relations.

Thus, in 1979, Deng launched what he called the "open door" policy, designating four special economic zones for foreign investors along the southern coast in Guangdong and Fujian provinces. He argued that foreign investment would help to create new jobs and bring in new technology, serving as "schools" for learning how to operate in a market economy. These zones were widely promoted but were not initially very successful in attracting much investment. In an attempt to encourage more FDI, in 1983, the Chinese state relaxed the restrictions that had limited foreign investment to joint ventures and agreed to allow wholly owned foreign operations.

Among the first effects of the urban reform process was rising prices. State firms began shifting their sales to the unregulated market where they could charge higher prices. Private producers followed suit. Officially, prices rose 6 percent in 1979 and 7 percent in 1980. Actual inflation was higher. This inflation undermined the wages of state workers and, in an attempt to head off worker opposition to the reforms, the state provided additional funds to state enterprises so that they could raise wages. This extra spending pushed the state budget into deficit and in 1981 the state began issuing bonds to raise funds for the first time since the early 1950s.[22]

The closure of some state enterprises as well as new state-imposed labor regulations in state-owned enterprises also led to unemployment. The state responded to this problem by intensifying its support for private and collective enterprises, in part because their activities were not dependent on state funds.

In 1981, with inflation and labor resistance to employment changes generating fears of social and economic instability, the state decided to bring its urban reform efforts to a temporary halt. It slowed down economic activity and reintroduced central control over state enterprise activity, especially over selling and pricing decisions.

State efforts to reform the rural economy began not long after the introduction of the urban reforms. Their aim was to boost agricultural production through market-based reforms. In the spring of 1979, the government raised prices for compulsory grain deliveries by 20 percent and offered a 50 percent premium for grain delivered above quotas. It also boosted prices of other agricultural products.[23] In addition, it reduced state restrictions on rural markets and increased legal limits on the size of private plots within the commune.[24]

In September 1980, the government took another major step in the reform process: it ordered the decollectivization of agricultural production. The decollectivization process involved a series of steps in which the commune-based system was replaced by a family-based household production system. By 1983 approximately 98 percent of all peasant households were operating according to the logic of this new system, using collective land to produce agricultural goods for sale on the market. While in theory the land was still public property, in reality it had become the private property of those families that had contracted for its use.[25] New government regulations issued in

1983 and 1984 allowed those in possession of contracted land to use wage workers for production or to rent out the land to tenant farmers. By the end of the 1980s those in possession of contracted land had full rights to rent it, sell it, or pass it on to their heirs.

The demise of the commune system also involved the transfer of political and economic power to new governmental entities. The new constitution of December 1982 gave the communes' previous political and administrative powers to newly created township and village governments. These governments also took possession of the communes' industrial assets, which were restructured as township and village enterprises (TVEs).

One of the big attractions of the Chinese reform strategy for progressives, especially outside of China, was the rise of TVEs. Left critiques of state socialism had focused on the undemocratic and wasteful consequences of the highly centralized control over, and top-down management of, state-owned enterprises. TVEs were seen as a hopeful alternative form of organization, in that they were said to be collectively organized and market oriented.

The number of TVEs grew fast, from 1.5 million in 1987 to 25 million in 1993.[26] By the latter year, TVEs were employing over 123 million workers, up from 28 million in 1978 (see table 4). However, these enterprises never functioned as vehicles for worker empowerment or socialist advancement. In actual fact, few are collectives involving worker decision making; they are really "private operations in disguise."[27] In many cases individual government leaders run them, appointing managers and directing the allocation of earnings. In some cases they are actually joint ventures, in which foreign capital maintains a controlling position through its domination of the board of directors. They can and do go bankrupt. It is common for many of the workers to be temporary, with management having power to hire and fire at will.[28]

In addition, worker earnings have remained low. This is not surprising insofar as the TVEs "fall outside many of the regulations designed to protect the rights and conditions of urban workers. Trade unions are usually absent or piecemeal in such workplaces, and their record on welfare, rights, and health and safety is very poor."[29] Studies have shown that "on average TVE workers earn basic wages which are lower than the minimum wage and must earn the rest through over-time and piece-rate quota bonuses. Even the basic wage is not guaran-teed since the minimum wage is set by local township authorities whose material interests—both institutionally and privately—are tied up in the maximization of profit."[30] Indeed, TVE "competitiveness and profit margins" are largely underwritten by the "abundant supply of dirt-cheap rural labor" freed up by the dissolution of the commune system and impoverishment of individual farm families.[31]

In terms of their contribution to employment, the TVEs peaked in absolute and relative terms in the mid-1990s. Since 1996, both the absolute number of TVE workers and their share of the total labor force have declined, although they retain a significant share of rural employment (see table 4). In large measure this trend is the result of new state policies that stress the benefits of privatization. One result of the decline in TVEs is that more and more rural workers (current-ly well over 100 million by most accounts) have been migrating on a seasonal basis to urban areas in search of employment. There, they make up a large pool of cheap labor power, which private enterprises use to discipline the urban industrial labor force.[32]

The changes in agricultural policy highlighted above produced big gains in agricultural output between 1978 and 1984. According to Meisner, this was "perhaps the most economically successful period in the history of Chinese agriculture."[33] The gross value of rural out-put, including that produced by the township and village industries, grew by an average annual rate of 9 percent in comparison to 4 percent in Mao's last decade. As a result, per capita rural incomes doubled over the 1978–84 period.[34]

While the Chinese government argued that its privatization and marketization policies were responsible for these gains, the real cred-it should go to the higher agricultural prices offered by the govern-ment as well as its shift of investment funds to support agriculture and rural-based light industry.[35] In fact, agricultural gains came to a halt by 1985. The end of the commune system led to the decay and collapse of the rural infrastructure and social support system. Grain production declined, and farmers, finding it difficult to support

themselves and their families, began abandoning the land for rural or
urban industrial work.[36]

THE REFORM PROCESS: STAGE II (1984–91)

The party's freeze on urban reforms and economic tightening during 1982–83 succeeded in stabilizing the urban economy. And,
encouraged by the early gains in rural production and incomes, the
state decided to renew, in fact accelerate, its urban reform efforts in
1984. This decision was based on the party's determination that
inflation and unemployment were largely due to the limited nature
of the prior urban reform efforts and that the best way to overcome
both problems was to push the reforms forward. They believed that
if state-owned firms and local governments were given more economic freedom then they would be better able to organize production so as to lower costs and prices. Meanwhile, new initiatives to
encourage the growth of private, especially foreign-owned enterprises would help to keep unemployment within acceptable limits.

Although the party initially presented market reforms as providing a mechanism for enhancing the efficiency and effectiveness of
central planning and the operation of state-owned enterprises, the
second stage of reform actually involved a shift in policy toward
greater reliance on market forces and non-state production. Thus,
while the Twelfth Congress of the Party held in 1982 gave economic
planning "primary" status and market regulation a "secondary" status, at the third plenum of the Twelfth Congress in 1984, the party
adopted the notion of a "planned commodity economy," thereby ele-
vating the status of market forces.[37]

More specifically, the new reforms involved a further reduction
in central control over and support for state enterprises. In the
past, state enterprises received all their funding from the state and,
in return, transferred all their revenue to the state. The new
reforms ended this relationship. Rather than receive state alloca-
tions of funds, state enterprises would now be expected to finance
their operations through retained earnings (after taxes) and bank
loans from the state banking system. "Since the loans bore interest

and were repayable, it was assumed that they would encourage factory directors to utilize scarce capital with greater prudence and in a more economically rational fashion, thereby mitigating the chronic problem of the overproduction of some goods while there were persistent shortages of other products."[38]

The state also changed its budgetary relationship with local and provincial governments. These units of government were now given the right to retain a greater share of the tax revenue and earnings they collected and greater freedom over how to use them. This was to further encourage them to pursue investments and organize the production of enterprises under their jurisdiction in response to market opportunities.

Having decided to rely on market forces to shape production and investment decisions, the state had little choice but to end state control over prices. An October 1984 party decree allowed the prices of most consumer and agricultural goods to move freely in response to market forces. The prices of most industrial products would also be allowed to move freely, but within a band set by state planners. Only the prices of basic industrial and essential industrial products like steel, coal, and oil would still be set by the central government.[39]

The party's tighter embrace of market forces also required significant new labor market reforms. These reforms were necessary to ensure that state managers would be free to pursue maximum profits in response to changing market conditions. Already, in 1982 the Chinese Communist Party had "abolished the right to strike in the new constitution."[40] But party proposals to end employment guarantees for state workers were an even more controversial reform.[41] A compromise was reached within the party which mandated that while workers already employed at state enterprises as of October 1985 would retain their job tenure and benefits, newly hired workers were to be hired under a contract system for a specific time limit.[42] Moreover, they could be fired if management felt that they were not sufficiently productive.

As one measure of how quickly China's reform process was promoting the commodification of labor, by 1984, regular state workers made up only 40 percent of China's industrial labor force (which also included rural industrial workers).[43] Hence, the relatively stable share of state enterprises in total manufacturing employment through the mid-1980s masked a real decline in the average employment security of state-enterprise workers.

State workers, not surprisingly, opposed these moves toward a two-tier labor force and increased managerial prerogatives. As Gerard Greenfield and Apo Leong explain:

> There was strong resistance by workers to the labor contract system, though in official discourse the failure to implement the Labor Contract Law of 1986 in state-owned and collective enterprises was attributed to bureaucratism and poor understanding of why or how it was to be done. Although managers acquired even greater powers in 1988 with official recognition of their power of dismissal, they did not overcome resistance to the labor contract system on the shop floor. In 1986 only six percent of state-owned enterprise (SOE) workers were placed under the contract system, increasing to a quarter of all SOE workers in 1994.[44]

Worker resistance to the new contract system was also reflected in a slowdown in labor productivity growth, as employed workers refused to give up their job security and labor force entrants continued to demand access to secure state-sector jobs.[45] As a result, "the reforms were considerably reinterpreted, amended and weakened, particularly by the trade unions, before they were introduced to the workplace."[46] New performance-based pay initiatives, for example, were only very partially implemented.[47]

Meanwhile, the state continued to place a high priority on foreign investment. In 1984, the territorial areas of the four original special economic zones were expanded and fourteen additional coastal cities were opened to foreign investment. In 1985 three large regions were similarly opened to foreign investment: the Pearl River delta, Min River delta, and Yangtze River delta. In essence the entire coastal area was opened to foreign investment.

This effort was justified by the alleged success of the Shenzhen zone in promoting export-oriented foreign investment, making it "the vanguard of urban reform" for the entire country. In reality, Shenzhen was far from a success.[48] There was alot of economic activity in the zone, most visibly state construction to build sites for foreign investors, especially from Hong Kong. However, while Hong Kong businesses did invest in the zone, their contribution was minimal. Operations, which took advantage of the region's low-cost labor force, did little to build industrial skills or transfer technology. They also did little to boost China's foreign exchange earnings. "Rather than exporting its products, some 70 percent of the goods produced in Shenzhen were sold on the Chinese domestic market, often illegally for foreign currencies. Moreover, most of what Shenzhen imported, either from abroad or from other parts of China, wasn't consumed within the zone itself but resold for illegal profits to buyers in the interior of China."[49]

Even when it became clear that Shenzhen was functioning primarily as a base for illegal private profit making, the state continued with its special zone strategy. In 1986, the government introduced new and more liberal regulations for foreign investment. These included lowering taxes and other costs of business, giving foreign companies more freedom to hire and fire workers, and making it easier for them to acquire foreign exchange.

In March 1987, Zhao Ziyang, then secretary general of the Chinese Communist Party, called for offering foreign investors new preferential conditions as part of his proposed coastal development strategy. In an October 1987 report to the Thirteenth National Congress of the Communist Party of China, entitled *Advance Along the Road of Socialism with Chinese Characteristics*, he declared that China "should enter the world economic arena more boldly" and that its aim should be to develop an "export-oriented economy."[50] Zhao's strategy received the support of the party congress.

As before, the reform effort almost immediately began generating serious economic imbalances and tensions. With enhanced freedom to pursue profits, state firms and TVEs raised their prices and began borrowing to boost their productive capacity. Local governments also began buying up and converting farmland into industrial use. The cost of construction materials soared as did the prices of investment goods and materials. This burst of demand triggered a sharp rise in imports, especially of basic inputs and machinery. China's balance of trade registered sizable deficits in 1985 and 1986, of $14.9 billion and $12.0 billion respectively.[51]

Inflation also became a major problem. After rising at an annual rate of approximately 8 percent over the years 1985–87, prices jumped by more than 18 percent in both 1988 and 1989. They rose even more, by as much as 30 percent, in Beijing and other large cities. The large increase in inflation again forced the government to raise state wages. This, in turn, produced a growing central budget deficit: a record $5.9 billion in 1986, a new record of over $6 billion in 1987, and yet another record deficit of over $9 billion in 1988.[52] These deficits were financed by state borrowing, which in turn added to inflationary pressures.

The seriousness of the problems of inflation, declining real wages, trade deficits, and budget deficits took several years to become apparent. Initially it appeared that the reforms had succeeded brilliantly. During 1980–89, China's real GDP grew at an annual average rate of 9.7 percent, tied with South Korea for the world's fastest rate of growth.

More direct evidence of success came from the generally acknowledged improvement in rural and urban living standards during the first few years of this phase of the reform process. As noted above, the rise in agricultural production during the early 1980s and establishment and growth of rural industries generated a rapid increase in rural incomes. This increase, coupled with the government's support for light industry and willingness to run budget and trade deficits, combined to ensure a growing demand for goods and services and a plentiful supply of those goods and services.

However, the collapse of the commune system and rising prices of agricultural inputs eventually put the squeeze on farm production, which began stagnating by the mid-1980s. Agricultural incomes, which grew by 15 percent per year during 1978–84, rose by only 5 percent annually over 1985–88, and by a mere 2 percent in 1989–91.[53] Rural industries, whose output had grown by an average annual rate of 37.7 percent between 1984–87, also faced growing hardships in the following years largely as a result of inflation and a shift in government policy toward urban industry.[54]

The inflation also hit urban workers hard. The government admitted that 20 percent of urban families suffered declines in their living standards in 1987.[55] An unpublished report of the All-China Federation of Trade Unions estimated that the average real income of China's urban population had fallen by 21 percent in the same year.[56] And, with inflation accelerating in the following years, poverty problems likely grew worse, especially for those employed in the state sector.

With trade and budget deficits, inflation, food shortages, and labor unrest growing, the government finally decided in late 1988 to halt its reform efforts and slow down the economy by tightening the money supply and reducing bank loans and investment. The economy went into recession in 1989. TVEs were especially hurt since they relied heavily on bank loans. Rural unemployment rose sharply and many of those unemployed began migrating to the cities in search of employment. Protests by urban workers against economic conditions also became increasingly common. In response, "the government took a tougher line":

> Premier Li Peng told the police to be vigilant against "social upheavals," while control of the media was tightened...as editors were told not to criticize the economic reforms, not to talk of political reform, and to be very careful about reporting incidents of industrial action against price increases in places like Poland.[57]

This history provides the context for the rise of China's democracy movement, the events of Tiananmen Square, and the political repression that followed, which especially targeted workers who had formed autonomous workers' federations in solidarity with students. The Chinese government maintained its tough political line and the economic status quo throughout 1990.

THE REFORM PROCESS: STAGE III (1991–PRESENT)

The economic slowdown once again helped restore economic stability, encouraging the government to resume its expansionary policies in 1991. And, in early 1992, Deng Xiaoping launched the next stage of China's reform process while on a month-long tour of southern China. During a visit to the special economic zone at Shenzhen, he declared that "as long as it makes money it is good for China."

The Fourteenth Party Congress, in October 1992, announced its determination to establish a "socialist market economy with Chinese characteristics."[58] Markets, of course, were already freely operating in China. The significant development in this stage of the reform process was that the party had now decided to abandon its long held commitment to state-owned enterprises as the central anchor of the Chinese economy.

As W. K. Lau explains: "The official SOE reform policy had been conceived in terms of revitalizing the majority of SOEs...by means of increasing SOE autonomy, managerial incentive creation, subjecting SOEs to increasing market discipline, state developmental intervention and the like."[59] However, the Chinese state had now decided to shrink the state sector, not simply by encouraging faster growth in the non-state sector, but by actually privatizing SOEs.

This step required a careful restatement of the party's earlier position that the state sector would play the leading role in the economy in order to maintain the socialist character of China's development:

> In November [1993], the third plenum of the Fourteenth [Party Congress] adopted a resolution on how to establish the 'socialist market economy.' In line with the Thirteenth Congress' position, the public sector would remain the 'principal part' of the economy. This would be achieved by it occupying a 'dominant position' in total assets, with the state economy playing a 'leading role' through holding 'controlling stakes' in enterprises in 'pillar industries' and the 'key enterprises' in 'basic industries.' In other words, private equity participation in all but military enterprises and SOEs producing 'exceptional products' was envisioned.[60]

The state's plan was to turn targeted large and medium state enterprises into limited liability or shareholding companies. Limited liability companies would have two to fifty shareholders. Shareholding companies would have more than fifty shareholders and could offer public issues. One hundred centrally run and 2,500 locally run state-owned enterprises were selected for the conversion, which was largely completed by late 1998.[61]

In late 1994, the privatization policy was extended under the slogan of "grasp the big and enliven the small." Under this policy, the state determined that it would maintain control over the 1,000 largest state-owned enterprises, while "all remaining state firms would be available for leasing or sale into private hands."[62] This privatization was "done de jure or de facto through transformation into so-called share-based co-operatives (SBC). In SBCs, shares are supposed to be sold to the enterprise's employees only (hence the 'cooperative' nature). The term 'employee' (zhigong), however, includes management, and in practice, profitable firms have mostly been privatized through management buyout, while workers are forced to take up unprofitable ones in order to save their jobs."[63]

Since 1995, the privatization of small SOEs has proceeded at a rapid pace. Ironically, this privatization drive picked up steam just when many left and progressive economists were celebrating the China experience as offering a new model for socialism. By the end of the 1990s, SOEs employed only 83 million people, representing just 12 percent of total employment and just over one-third of urban employment. Their contribution to GDP had declined to only 38 percent.[64]

As a result of these developments, the joint-stock company was becoming the dominant form of enterprise organization. For example:

> At the end of 1996 4,300 SOEs had been converted into joint stock companies. In 1997 there were over 9,200 joint stock companies in China including start-up firms and those transformed from existing companies (both SOEs and rural enterprises); 107 of them ranked among China's largest 500 industrial enterprises and 62 ranked among China's largest 500 service enterprises. Their average net fixed assets was 500 billion yuan, representing over 20% of the total for all industrial SOEs.[65]

Still, the process of privatization continued. In September 1999, the Fourth Plenum of the Fifteenth Party Congress expanded the "let go of policy" to include medium as well as small state-owned enterprises. In July 2000, even the Beijing city government announced that state and collective ownership would be phased out in all small and medium-sized SOEs within three years.[66] As of 2001, state enterprises accounted for only 15 percent of total manufacturing employment and less than 10 percent of employment in domestic trade (see table 3).

The Chinese Communist Party defended this privatization process by adopting the neoliberal economic argument that private firms are inherently more efficient than state enterprises. It argued that past economic problems were due to the failure of state enterprises to fully orient their production and investment decisions towards market-based profit-making activities. They continued to employ too many workers, produce inefficiently, and remain overly dependent on bank debt and state subsidies to sustain their operations.

However, reviews of the theoretical and empirical literature on privatization have concluded that no such blanket endorsement of private over state enterprise is warranted. Rather, the consensus (at least outside hard-core neoliberal circles) is that the effects of privatization on efficiency depend on market conditions in the relevant industries (including financial and technological conditions), the quality of private corporate governance, and the degree of inefficiency and corruption in the privatization process itself (e.g., in the pricing of assets sold off).[67] Moreover, the vaunted "efficiency" of private over public enterprises is often due to the former's unencumbered pursuit of private profit, whereas state firms are often charged with additional economic and political goals such as employment and welfare provision, and promotion of fixed capital formation, that have a high social priority even if they are not profitable for the firms undertaking them. Indeed, one detailed comparison of China's industrial SOEs and non-SOEs over the 1978–2000 period found that the profitability gap between them was fully explained by the higher tax rate on and greater capital intensity of the SOEs, both of which reflected specific government priorities and/or discrimination against SOEs.[68]

In reality, privatization in China has been driven by the exercise of class power and the nature of the reform process itself. The basic class dynamic is one in which "Communist cadres use their party cards to 'borrow' state assets to set themselves up as capitalists, while under the banner of 'socialism with Chinese characteristics,' they wield a club to break the workers' 'iron rice bowl'—their right to employment, housing, food rations and other benefits."[69] This "asset stripping" by enterprise or party insiders can take place in a number of different ways, including fraud, selective transfers of assets to independent subsidiaries (domestic or in Hong Kong), channeling firm subsidies toward personal uses (children's tuition, entertainment and travel expenses, for example), tax avoidance and evasion, undervaluation of state assets when setting up joint ventures, opportunistic use of share-holding enterprise forms (joint-stock and/or shareholding cooperative forms), illegal sale of state assets or their legal sale at undervalued prices, and/or bad debts and bank lending practices.[70]

Regardless of the means, asset stripping turns state property into capital assets that can be used to exploit the freed-up labor power, replicating what Marx termed "primary capital accumulation," although this time in the name of the "socialist market economy." Russell Smyth cites "'rough estimates' of the daily loss of state assets at between 100 million yuan and 300 million yuan."[71] Other studies provide additional support for the seriousness of the problem:

> In 1994 the People's Bank of China prepared a survey entitled 'Research Report on the Loss of State-Owned Assets' based on a sample of 50,000 state-run industrial enterprises. It found that just 5% of state-owned capital increased in value, while 62% decreased in value and 23% lost all of its value entirely. According to a separate survey of 124,000 SOEs conducted by the National Administrative Bureau for State-Owned Property in 1994, asset losses and unac-countable expenses amounted to 11.6% of total assets in the sample firms. The situation has got much worse since the Fifteenth Congress in September 1997.[72]

This outcome is not just the result of personal greed, but also an inex-orable result of the alienation of the party from its purported working-class base. The more market reforms were pursued, the more the party "antagonized working people, and thus the more acutely it felt the need to restore private property so that its privileges could be passed on to the bureaucrats' children."[73] As noted by Eva Cheng, the party's push "for capitalism in all but name" has been "supported zealously by the military, provincial and local bureaucrats whose ability to pur-sue their private gains has been much enhanced by the material resources provided by sweeping fiscal decentralization."[74]

Alongside these class dynamics, the effects of the reform process on the financial stability of the state sector and banking system were also a crucial factor leading to party endorsement of privatization. In the pre-reform fiscal system, government revenue derived mainly from a simple indirect tax on, and the direct transfer of earnings from, state-owned enterprises. From 1957–78, state industry accounted for 75 percent of all fiscal income.[75] State planners would then allocate funds to enterprises for production and investment according to plan priorities and in support of social welfare policies.

However, the budget system could not keep up with the reform process. Under market socialism, state enterprises no longer automatically transferred all their revenue to the central government. They did continue to pay taxes, but the amount was limited by their declining earnings. One important reason for the decline in earnings was the reform process. By opening markets to competing private enterprises that were free of the many employment and social welfare obligations of state-owned enterprises, the party undermined the state sector's monopoly power and profitability.[76]

While state firms faced growing financial difficulties, the private sector enjoyed rapid growth. By 1995 it accounted for 40.4 percent of non-agricultural employment, 35 percent of registered capital, 33.8 percent of industrial output, 45.1 percent of retail sales, and 47.7 percent of exports.[77] Moreover, the private sector enjoyed especially favorable tax rates. As a result, while the private sector accounted for roughly 40 percent of national economic activity, it contributed only 11.4 percent of tax payments.[78] As a consequence, fiscal revenue as a share of GDP fell from approximately 35 percent in 1978 to less than 11 percent in 1996.[79] The state thus found itself with a growing budget deficit. This development was especially troubling for social stability, since the central government, as part of its reform effort, was committed to assuming responsibility for various social welfare functions, including health care and unemployment insurance.

State-owned enterprises also found themselves increasingly short of funds. One reason was their crushing tax burden. Between 1982 and 1996, the state taxed away 86 percent of total state sector net income.[80] This situation forced state enterprises to increase their reliance on bank loans. However, the decline in state enterprise earnings meant that state banks were extending more and more credit to enterprises that were increasingly unable to repay their debts. This put China's banking system at risk:

> The Xinhua News Agency has reported that the central bank's governor, Dai Xianglong, admits that non-performing loans (NPLs) account for 26.6 percent of total lending by China's top four state-owned commercial banks. As of the end of September last year [2001], NPLs held by these financial institutions totaled 1.8 trillion yuan (US$217 billion)....Things may be worse than they sound because China substantially understates its NPLs relative to international accounting standards. State-owned banks classify a loan as non-performing only if interest payments have not been paid for two years....By contrast, the international standard classifies bad loans as those that have not been serviced after three months. According to Ernst & Young, nearly half of all loans made by Chinese banks may never be repaid.[81]

Although aware of the problem, the authorities were reluctant to order a halt to the loans for fear that state-sector bankruptcies would intensify the brewing fiscal crisis and create a potentially more dangerous unemployment problem. Thus, the reform process created instability in the state sector, which was transmitted to both the central government's fiscal budget and the state banking system.[82]

The party found privatization to be the most attractive response to this situation. For one thing, sales of state enterprises would generate desperately needed state revenue. Moreover, newly privatized enterprises were expected to be less dependent on the state banking system for operating funds. The city of Shenyang, "once a major heavy industrial base on the Chinese planned economy," offers a good example of the scope of the resulting privatization process. "The city government formed a joint venture with a Hong Kong–based subsidiary of a British investment bank and put 126 SOEs and 18 industrial groups into its portfolio to sell to domestic and foreign investors."[83]

Similar dynamics also led to the privatization of most TVEs. As the reform process proceeded in the early 1990s, the TVEs lost many of their earlier advantages. As Samuel P. S. Ho, Paul Bowles and Xiaoyuan Dong explain:

The banks, the main source of funds for TVEs expansion in the mid-late 1980s, came under increasing pressure to operate on more business-like lines and to scrutinize loan applications more carefully. The deepening of enterprise reforms in the state sector further reduced the organizational advantages which TVEs had enjoyed over SOEs in the area of enterprise autonomy. Moreover, the markets for many products produced by TVEs had shifted from sellers' to buyers' markets; the degree of market competition facing TVEs intensified and the macroeconomy became sluggish. This came at a bad time for TVEs which had invested heavily in the 1993–94 period, largely financed by bank loans, following the impetus given to the economy by Deng's southern tour.[84]

Equally devastating for TVEs, with new opportunities to profit from private production, many managers began illegally transferring TVE assets or products to private enterprises where they could earn greater returns. This asset stripping accelerated in the mid-1990s after the party committed to the privatization of small state enterprises. Convinced that "their enterprises would be sold to them sooner or later...managers [believed that] the more the enterprise's assets went down, the lower would be the price they needed to pay when the local government finally decided to sell the enterprise."[85]

Faced with declining profits and deindustrialization, township and village officials took their cue from state officials and began a rapid sell off of TVEs beginning in 1996. More often than not, township and village officials sold the TVEs under their control to the individuals that had managed them, believing that that this was the most effective way to ensure an end to the asset stripping that had helped to encourage the privatization in the first place.[86]

As a result of these developments, China's economic future now depends on the performance of privately owned enterprises, a reality acknowledged, if not welcomed, by the Communist Party. In 2002, the party opened its membership to private entrepreneurs. And, in December 2003, it recommended that the National People's Congress amend the constitution to provide a new and stronger legal foundation for private property, placing it "on an equal footing with public property."

Privatization was not the only strategy forced on the central authorities by the contradictions of its reform effort. As suggested by the

Shenyang example, the state also redoubled its effort to attract FDI. Attracting foreign investors was important in part because not many domestic investors had sufficient resources to afford shares in the large and medium-sized firms scheduled for privatization. Foreign enterprises were also thought likely to help promote the desired profit-maximizing behavior throughout the economy. They were also thought able to generate the exports needed to cover China's rising trade deficit.

The Chinese government implemented a number of policies to attract FDI, including opening up new geographic areas and industries to this investment. As desired by the government, most FDI—approximately 90 percent between 1986 and 1999—has so far been in the coastal areas.[87] The initial foreign investment came largely from overseas Chinese; but starting in the early 1990s, U.S., European, and Japanese investors have greatly increased their share.[88] To this point, most FDI has been in manufacturing. However, there appears to be a specialization based on the nationality of the investor. As Elissa Braunstein and Gerald Epstein explain:

> Investors from the Chinese Diaspora of Hong Kong and Taiwan, etc. are at one end, investing primarily in labor-intensive, low-wage exporting firms; [at the other end are] firms from Japan investing in intermediate goods products and higher quality products for the Japanese market; and U.S. and European firms primarily investing in firms they hope will sell to the Chinese market. Of course, U.S. firms are well known to hire low-wage firms on a contract basis to produce goods for export.[89]

China's success in attracting FDI and the importance of that investment to the Chinese economy during this stage of the reforms can be highlighted in a number of different ways. Table 2, for example, shows the rapid growth in FDI in dollars and as a percentage of gross investment, beginning in the first half of the decade of the 1990s. As a result of this investment, the share of foreign manufacturing affiliates in total manufacturing sales grew rapidly and steadily from 2.3 percent in 1990, to 14.3 percent in 1995, and to 31.3 percent in 2000 (table 5).

Perhaps most important, foreign investors, with government encouragement, have helped to transform China into an export-led economy. The ratio of exports to GDP climbed steadily over the decade of the 1990s, from 16 percent in 1990 to over 26 percent by 2002 (see table 1). And, as table 6 illustrates, these exports were increasingly produced by foreign-funded enterprises; they now account for over 50 percent of the country's total exports. As a part of this process, the share of manufactured exports in total exports rose from 48.6 percent in 1980, to 55.7 percent in 1990, and 85.5 percent in 1996.[90] As a result of this development, China's economic growth is now becoming increasingly dependent on the export activities of foreign transnational corporations.

This transformation was intensified by the East Asian crisis of 1997–98. The crisis led to stagnation in FDI and threatened to trigger a slowdown in the Chinese economy with serious repercussions as far as employment and social stability were concerned. In response, the Chinese government worked hard to reassure foreign investors and provide new incentives for a renewal of investment. Above all this required a sustained effort to join the World Trade Organization (WTO). China succeeded, becoming a member in December 2001.

This achievement is likely to lead to a further dismantling of the state sector and consolidation of foreign production as the leading force in the Chinese economy. As UNCTAD explains:

> The Chinese economy has a dualistic industrial structure. While it has a highly competitive labor-intensive, export-oriented manufacturing sector dominated by FFEs [foreign funded enterprises], it also has a fairly traditional capital-intensive industrial sector dominated by State-owned enterprises (SOEs), as well as an agricultural sector that enjoys a relatively high degree of government support and protection. Although the SOEs account for about half of China's exports, their sales are, on balance, directed primarily at domestic markets. The SOE sector has been undergoing transformation and restructuring for several years, but the reform process is far from complete. Thus a rapid dismantling of trade barriers and removal of subsidies could expose SOEs to foreign competition, which could undermine their export performance, as well as lead to a surge in imports.[91]

The likely result of this intensified foreign competition is either the bankruptcy of a large segment of the state sector or its privatization.

And, with massive imports, the Chinese government would also be forced to promote an even greater reliance on exports. Given the structure of the Chinese economy, this would no doubt mean the further dominance of foreign-owned enterprises.

CONCLUSION

As we have seen, the Chinese economy has undergone a reform process delineated by three different stages. The first stage involved a weakening of central planning with the aim of creating a new, more efficient market socialist economy. The second involved privileging the market over planning. The third has led to the privileging of private enterprise over state enterprises, and increasingly foreign enterprises and markets over domestic ones. This reform process highlights the slippery slope of market reform. Once the path of pro-market reforms was embarked upon, each subsequent step in the reform process was largely driven by tensions and contradictions generated by the reforms themselves. This dynamic appears to verify recent Marxist theoretical criticisms of market socialist models.[92]

Our analysis of China's reforms also contradicts those progressives who, while downplaying explicit references to socialism, continue to view China as a model of national development. For these progressives, the contrast between China's successes and the reversals in the East Asian "miracle" countries shows that state-interventionist economic policies still work better than neoliberalism. But as we have seen, China's reform program has undermined the viability of state planning and direction of economic activity, thereby encouraging the adoption of a growth model increasingly dependent on foreign capital and exports—the same kind of growth model whose contradictions were revealed by the 1997–98 East Asian crisis.[93]

In sum, regardless of intentions, the Chinese Communist Party launched a process of economic transformation that has created an economy that has little to do with socialism. And for leftists to identify it as such is to create confusion about what socialism really means, thereby strengthening the ideological position of those that oppose it.

3

Contradictions of China's Transformation: Domestic

Many progressives agree that China is not a socialist country, but argue that its controlled process of transformation has been a success, having produced rapid industrial growth and a rising standard of living for the great majority of Chinese. The reality, however, is that the marketization, privatization, and increasing foreign domination of China's economy have generated growing tensions and contradictions that have already undermined economic stability and imposed unacceptably high costs on China's working people.

UNSTABLE ECONOMIC DYNAMICS

China's current instabilities can be traced not only to the inherent tensions and contradictions in capitalist accumulation but also to the starting point of the reform process. Deng launched his program of market reform on an economic structure that had been shaped by Mao's concern for defense and broad-based industrialization. Mao wanted to make sure that most regions were self-contained industrial networks; this produced national duplication of industrial facilities. Deng's decentralization efforts, which encouraged firms and local governments to undertake investment and production in the context of a market environment, were supposed to overcome this "inefficiency" by promoting more specialization, thereby boosting productivity and growth. These efforts received support from a new financial policy which encouraged banks to make "interest-bearing loans to enterprises rather than non-repayable grants...with the aim of encouraging enterprises to use their funds more efficiently."[1] There was, after all, "no formal requirement for banks to continue lending to loss-making enterprises."[2]

The result of these new policies was that state banks, for reasons of political expediency and corruption, more or less passively accommodated the credit demands of state enterprises and local governments eager to expand their existing industrial activities and/or undertake new ones in the hopes of gaining wealth. Investment and production thus "functioned in a system of 'soft budget constraints'" in which "demands of enterprises (or provinces) or the flow of investable funds supplied by the banks were not always subject to a rigorous risk/incentive calculus."[3] The hypothetical power of banks "to restrict credit to loss-making enterprises and to require their restructuring" was "rarely undertaken" in practice, so that bankruptcy "pose[d] no serious threat to enterprise managers."[4]

Rather than produce a more specialized and efficient economy, this dynamic only reinforced China's "duplicative industrial structure by allowing every production branch at both the central and local levels continued expanded reproduction in the extensive mode."[5] One example: "As of 1997, 22 out of 30 provinces wanted to have their own automobile industry, such that there were altogether 122 whole-vehicle assembly lines with a combined annual output of only 1.5 m vehicles, 80% of the plants produced less than 1,000, and only 6 plants more than 50,000 vehicles annually."[6]

State-owned enterprises were even given extra incentives to increase production and "engage in extra-plan activities." Supplementary fiscal resources were also supplied to local governments to promote "socioeconomic developments in their jurisdiction."[7] Not surprisingly, enterprises and governmental units raced to take advantage of these subsidies and their new freedom to pursue profit. "State-owned enterprises were too eager to increase their investment—

managers and workers could get higher remuneration if the projects succeeded, but they would lose almost nothing if they failed. Local governments, which had also been given more autonomy in the usage of retained tax revenues, also favored high economic growth. They often forced the state banks to provide funding to the enterprises."8

All of this investment did, of course, accelerate economic growth. But it also created a massive excess demand for goods and services, triggering inflation and economic instability. This forced the government to slow the economy and bring a halt to the first stage of the reform process in 1981–83. The reform drive was restarted, in a second stage, in 1984. But once again growing inflation and economic instability forced the government to bring it to a halt in 1988–90. In short, "overexpansion of credit" had become "a continuing tendency...giving a 'stop-go' character to financial macro-management."9 The general "proliferation of banking institutions and the emphasis on expanding the quantity of funds" also contributed to this problem, given "the weakness of central control over an increasingly diverse and decentralized financial system."10

The government launched the third stage in the reform process in 1991. As before, the economy expanded rapidly with GDP growing at a record 14.2 percent in 1992, 13.5 percent in 1993, and 12.6 percent in 1994 (see table 1). But the unplanned nature of the growth process again triggered a massive inflation. Consumer prices rose, according to official figures, at a record 14.7 percent in 1993, 24.1 percent in 1994, and 17.1 percent in 1995 (see table 7).

With the inflationary spiral rising to new heights, the government searched for new ways to regain control over the allocation and use of resources. It introduced new tax laws to reduce the flow of resources to local governments in favor of the central government. It also took steps to recentralize the banking system. In 1994, it created three policy banks, which were to operate under the supervision of the central government. Finally, the central government reorganized the People's Bank of China (China's central bank), replacing provincial branches with regional branches in an effort to reduce provincial government intervention in lending activity.

However, the reform process did more than generate inflation, it also undermined the stability and viability of the state sector itself. As discussed in chapter 2, state enterprises found their earnings insufficient to sustain their operations, especially given that the reform process had lowered their profitability. This left them increasingly dependent on state bank loans for funds. And, as the state banks continued to lend to loss-making SOEs, they accumulated more and more delinquent loans on their books—a problem accentuated by the banks' tendency to provide new loans to refinance both the old loans and to cover new SOE losses.[11] As a result, the overall SOE debt-equity ratio rose from 23 percent in 1980 to 440 percent in 1998, while the ratio of non-performing loans to total loans in the state banks (conservatively estimated) rose to about 24 percent just before the 1997–98 East Asian crisis, and to at least 29 percent immediately thereafter.[12]

The central government tried to deal with these loan problems through the creation of asset management companies (AMCs) that were to absorb bad loans and sell them at a discount; but the market for these recycled debts turned out to be so soft that the AMCs were forced to convert them into stock in the bankrupt companies, which was then carried on AMC books. In this way, the potential write-offs involved were merely shifted to the People's Bank of China, which stands behind the AMCs.[13] Thus, the government has so far been unable to fashion a workable response to growing state-sector production and financial problems.

THE SOCIAL CONSEQUENCES
OF ECONOMIC REFORM

The Chinese economy now operates largely according to capitalist logic. This is reflected not only in the country's industrial structure that is increasingly defined by the operations of private, profit-making firms, but also in the accompanying transformation in the social relations and realities that shape the working and living conditions of the majority of Chinese working people. For example, the dismantling of the state sector has led to severe problems of unemployment. From 1995 through 1999, the number of state-owned industrial enterprises fell from approximately 100,000 to 60,000.[14] This decline translated into massive layoffs of state-sector workers. For example, from 1996 to 2001, some 36 million state-enterprise workers were laid off; over the same period collective firms laid off 17 million workers.[15]

Despite these large layoffs, the government claims that the urban unemployment rate rose from only 2.9 to 3.1 percent over the period 1995–2000 (table 7). However, its figures are severely biased downward. First, the government's measure of unemployment seriously underestimates the unemployment among rural residents and rural-urban migrants.[16] Second, it does not include workers who are laid off by state enterprises. These workers are not counted as unemployed. Rather they are classified as in a state of *xiagang* (off post) and continue to be listed with their enterprise. The percentage of state workers listed as *xiagang* has grown dramatically. According to Ching Kwan Lee:

> In a survey of redundant workers in 17 provinces, it was found that annual *xia-gang* rate increased steadily from 0.7 percent in 1988—when managers were first given the power to 'optimize' labor utilization—to 10 percent in 1994. But in 1995, at the time of heightened implementation of labor contracts, the rate skyrocketed to 23.8 percent and then to 35.8 percent in 1996.[17]

In sum, the official unemployment rate remains low because only "sacked workers aged up to 50 (for men) or 45 (for women) are officially classified as unemployed. Millions of others are neither *xiagang* nor sacked but without a job because their enterprises have simply ceased operation."[18]

The Social and Economic Policy Institute, an independent research group in Hong Kong, attempted to correct these shortcomings. Its estimates of the actual urban unemployment rate, shown in table 8, reveal a substantial and growing difference between official and real rates for the period 1993–98. Other analysts suggest an even higher real urban unemployment rate. For example, the "Central Bank governor, Dai Xianglong, estimated that in the first half of 1996, 7–8 percent, or 12–14 million, of the urban workforce was unemployed."[19] Rene Ofreneo cites a figure of roughly 13 percent, while an even higher estimate of 17–20 percent has been circulated by the International Labor Organization.[20]

Chinese workers have every reason to fear being laid off or unemployed. The *xiagang* workers in theory "still receive a portion of their former salaries and still have government housing," but for many workers these promises have not been kept. The rest of the unemployed "subsist on benefits of less than $10 a month."[21] According to the *Times of India*, the Chinese government admitted that:

> it faces a 'grim' problem of unemployment which appears likely to spiral into the country's worst ever joblessness crisis. The situation is considered so severe that it "could well undermine social stability," vice minister of labor and social security Wang Dongjin said, quoted by the state-run *China Daily*….The unusually frank admissions in a country which has traditionally claimed improbably low rates of joblessness follow weeks of industrial unrest centered around China's ailing northeastern industrial heartland. Many of the demonstrators in [what] have been among the biggest protests to hit the country in years were laid-off workers from inefficient state firms, a sector many economists expect to suffer even more following China's recent entry to the WTO.[22]

The reform process has also led to worsening income inequality. The Gini coefficient for household income in China rose from 0.33 in 1980, to 0.40 in 1994, and to 0.46 in 2000. The last figure surpasses the degree of inequality in Thailand, India, and Indonesia.[23] Most observers suspect that China's Gini coefficient now exceeds 0.50, placing its income inequality near Brazilian and South African levels.[24]

While most Chinese workers struggle to make ends meet, a small minority of petit bourgeois and bourgeois Chinese pursue lifestyles similar to upper-income U.S. citizens, complete with suburban upscale housing, luxury automobiles, gourmet cuisine, and high-fashion clothing and jewelry.[25] The Chinese government now uses May Day to pay tribute to the wealthy exploiters, as in 2002, when the All-China Federation of Trade Unions awarded medals "to the heads of four privately owned companies" while "another 17 businessmen were declared 'model workers' in the northwestern province of Shaanxi, where Mao once made his revolutionary headquarters."[26]

Women workers have been especially hard hit by the reform process. Women make up around 60 percent of workers laid off from SOEs, even though women account for only about 40 percent of the labor force.[27] In addition, the average duration of female unemployment tends to be longer than for males, as "75% of unemployed Chinese women are still in search of jobs after one year, compared with less than 50% of their male counterparts."[28]

Those still employed have been increasingly crowded into low-wage service jobs (janitorial and maid work, restaurant serving, for example), while the higher paying positions in industry and management are reserved for men. Even within job categories, pay discrimination against women is increasingly prevalent, and the size of the male-female wage gap (controlling for job characteristics) is much larger in the more liberalized (foreign-funded) firms than in the SOEs.[29] For those women who do find jobs in manufacturing, the reward is often backbreaking and dangerous toil at paltry wages—especially in the intensely competitive light-export sector.[30] More than a few women (estimates range from the tens to the hundreds of thousands) are captured by a growing black market for female labor (and brides)—a market underwritten not only by rural poverty and the demand for cheap labor power but also by the disproportionate abortion rate for female fetuses (in rural China six boys are born for every five girls).[31]

The growing deterioration of working conditions for Chinese workers may be the most important indicator of the bankruptcy of the Chinese reform process. Writing about these conditions, Tim Pringle observes:

> Abuses of Chinese workers' rights have been widely documented both inside and outside China over the past five years. Forced overtime, illegal working hours, unpaid wages, and dreadful health and safety conditions are commonplace. The general pace of work has increased dramatically as competition forces the prioritizing of order deadlines and production targets over safe and dignified working environments. "There is no such thing as an eight-hour day in China anymore," explained a private employment agency in Shulan, northeast China.[32]

According to the *New York Times*, "China has emerged as Asia's leading exporter of manufactured goods to the United States, but the workers who produce those goods are victims of a surge in fatal respiratory, circulatory, neurological and digestive-tract diseases like those American and European workers suffered at the dawn of the industrial age."[33] China's State Administration of Work Safety reported over 140,000 fatalities from workplace accidents in 2002, up from 100,000 two years earlier. The number of serious industrial injuries is no doubt much higher, but difficult to determine given the large number of incidents "left out of the official count either because the boss does not have insurance, or because workers were not hired legally, or because officials are under pressure to show that they have safety under control."[34]

The destruction of the communes and transformation of state enterprises have also meant that most working people have lost their social safety net, including pensions, housing, health care, and increasingly even primary and secondary education. For example, SOEs no longer provide pension benefits. Individual workers are now supposed to be served by a nationally organized system funded by worker, state, and employer contributions. By 1997, 78 percent of SOE employees and 95 percent of SOE retirees were to be covered by this national system. Tragically, because of its fiscal crisis, the state does not have sufficient funds to ensure adequate pensions.[35]

State enterprises also no longer provide housing support for new workers. Existing workers are told that they must pay market rents or buy their existing houses (with the support of credit from government institutions), if they want to continue living in them.[36]

SOEs also no longer provide health care to their employees. As with pensions, enterprise-based health care is to be replaced by a national system, supported by tripartite funding. However, as was true with pensions, the state does not have adequate revenue to provide even minimal health care. The growing number of workers "falling ill or suffering injuries on the job" are thus increasingly "fending for themselves with little or no health insurance."[37] In rural areas, the dissolution of the communes has also led to a collapse of public health care. "Huge numbers of China's 800 million rural residents are in a medical free fall, as the once-vaunted system of 'barefoot doctors' and free rural clinics has disintegrated over the last decade."[38] As a result, "Farmers in most parts of the country have difficulties gaining access to doctors or obtaining medicines or medical treatment."[39]

Nationwide, public health-care coverage declined from 90 percent of the population in 1978 to 4 percent in 1997.[40] "Today medical care in China is almost entirely a matter of cash from individual patients, and there is no public health insurance for the poor."[41] Accordingly, "the World Health Organization now rates China last among developing countries in terms of equal access to medical care."[42] As with employment restructuring, inequality in healthcare access (including maternity-related services, and treatment for occupational illnesses and injuries) has hit working-class women especially hard.[43]

The 2003 SARS crisis may offer the clearest illustration of the extent of the collapse of the Mao-era social welfare system.[44] But this debacle had been foreshadowed by the failure, of both government authorities and China's new free market in medical services, to respond to the country's worsening tuberculosis and HIV epidemics.[45] In fact, the collapse of public health services and growing poverty contributed to both problems, most tragically in the case of HIV, which was transmitted like wildfire through the selling of blood by immiserated rural workers. A *Guardian* reporter chronicles the connection between the reform process and the contemporary health crisis in China as follows:

> The provision of health services and social security to the mass of the population was perhaps the Chinese revolution's single most important achievement. But even at the height of the communist system there was never a national health service. The provision of medical care derived from a work unit—a factory, a school, a people's commune—that had the responsibility to take care of its workers and their families. It was an arrangement that covered most people, but with Deng Xiaoping's move to a market economy, the system was doomed....Economic liberalization meant the end of most of those work units: state industries are closing down, agricultural communes were disbanded long ago and agriculture has been privatized. Nothing has taken their place, and the services the units used to provide have lapsed. Responsibility for public health rests with local authorities which do not appear to have either the funds or the interest to maintain it. Even in the cities, where two decades of economic reforms have brought a general rise in living

standards, the burden of medical care is now largely a private responsibility that many can't afford....The SARS outbreak has reminded the Chinese of what has been lost over more than two decades of sustained economic growth, as they discover that dilapidated public health services are in no shape to fight an epidemic, or even to report one consistently.[46]

The same basic forces underpin a similar development in China's education system. As "Chinese schools have become increasingly privatized, they charge the parents steeper fees."[47] In fact, a rapid growth in urban elite private schools has taken place since the 1980s, with foreign investors playing a critical role.[48] Rising school fees and low incomes "are keeping an increasing number of children out of the classroom," especially in rural areas.[49] With the central government having "largely stopped subsidizing primary education a decade ago...education is increasingly a luxury item in China's poorest villages, purchased only when finances allow—and far more often for boys than for girls."[50] In some villages, only 20 percent of girls and 40 percent of boys attend school. There are entire provinces where less than half of the girls attend any school at all—and many who enter drop out before completing the elementary level.[51]

Not surprisingly, the effects of the destruction of the social safety net have not been gender neutral. Women have generally been called upon to carry a heavier domestic load, which then hampers their ability to find acceptable employment in China's increasingly deregulated labor market. As Ching Kwan Lee explains:

> In the reform period, the retreat of enterprise paternalism and the commodification of services means that reproductive responsibilities are privatized, that workers must either pay for services like child care, canteen meals and medical care, or resort as much as possible to the unpaid labor of women in the household....[As a result], it is not surprising to find that market opportunities for second jobs or job changes are also biased against women both because they have not accumulated as many marketable skills as their male counterparts and because their heavier domestic responsibilities deprive them of both the flexibility of time and geographical mobility required for second jobs or non-state sector jobs.[52]

WIDENING FAULT LINES

The negative social consequences of China's economic reforms have not only devastated the lives of uncountable numbers of Chinese. By undermining domestic purchasing power, they tend to reinforce the destructive dynamics of the reform process, thereby further extending and deepening the misery. Those left without jobs because of the dismantling of the state sector have been forced to greatly reduce their consumption. Even those who find new work, normally in the domestic private or urban collective sector, tend to earn lower wages, which limits their expenditures. Moreover, because most workers now need to finance their own health care and pensions, many have been forced to increase their savings, again at the expense of consumption.

The rural economy has not been immune to these trends. As *The Economist* explains, "the incomes of most rural residents (who account for 65 percent of the population) have been stagnating for the past four years [1998–2001]."[53] One government-proposed solution has been to move peasants out of farming and into other sectors. But rural industry has been facing declines and shedding workers. And, the urban areas have been unable to generate sufficient jobs to keep urban unemployment under control, let alone absorb additional flows of surplus labor from rural areas. As a result, the purchasing power of the majority of rural people (and of rural-urban migrants) has stagnated.[54]

The relative stagnation of mass working-class demand combined with the vastly expanded industrial base created by earlier investments in plant and equipment have created a crisis of excess capacity, especially in consumer durable goods industries. For example, in 1995, the capacity utilization rate was 44.3 percent in the motor vehicles industry, 46.1 percent in the color TV industry, 54.5 percent in the bicycle industry, 50.4 percent in the refrigerator industry.[55]

As noted by Bertell Ollman, such overproduction problems are a definite sign that China's economy has fallen under the sway of the exploitative and anarchic dynamics of capital accumulation.[56] "The earning power of China's notoriously low-paid workers (with relatively few workers making more than $60 a month) has kept consumption within China lagging far behind the rapidly expanding output of China's factories and workshops, and the growth of foreign markets, as impressive as that has been, has simply not been enough to take up the slack."[57] Liu Yufan draws the same sensible conclusion: "Overproduction and underconsumption are two ends of the same stick, and the name of the stick is capitalism."[58]

Another sign that overproduction has taken hold in China is the shift from inflation to deflation. Consumer prices rose at an annual rate of over 24 percent in 1994. By 1996 they were rising at a rate of only 8.3 percent (table 7). Beginning in the second quarter of 1998 the retail price index fell below zero for 22 consecutive months. While domestic imbalances generated the downward trend in prices, the Asian financial crisis, which produced a decline in exports and FDI, no doubt worsened deflationary pressures. In the case of exports, their growth rate fell from 21 percent in 1997 to only 0.5 percent in 1998 (see table 1). Prices did rise slightly in 2000 and 2001; but they fell again in 2002 (table 7).

The Chinese government, worried that sustained deflation might cause a massive collapse of the state industrial and financial sector, responded with several initiatives designed to boost demand. It cut interest rates beginning in May 1996 to stimulate borrowing and spending. This did not prove successful and the government made more aggressive moves. In 1998 it greatly increased its spending.[59] It continued heavy deficit spending in 1999 and 2000. The government also began slowly refocusing its spending away from infrastructure construction and towards social welfare programs, especially for health and pensions for workers being laid off by state companies, as well as research and development. Finally, it supported a significant loosening of controls on the expansion of bank credit.

While these initiatives succeeded in maintaining (officially measured) real growth at or above 7 percent per year (see table 1), they have done little to overcome underlying economic instabilities. Not only did deflation return in 2002, but the extra spending has added to the state's growing debt problems. The government claims that the public debt load remains under control. "As a ratio to GDP, China's fiscal deficit and outstanding debts in 1999 were respectively 1.7 percent and around 10 percent, well below the safety levels of 3 percent and 60 percent."[60] But things are not as positive as they may seem. First the government's definition of deficits remains problematic. For example, before 1994, the government recorded the issuance of public debts as part of budget revenue, thereby vastly undercounting the deficit. In addition, it was not until 2000 that the government started counting interest payments as a budgetary expenditure. Adjusting for this latter change alone brings the 2000 budget deficit to 2.9 percent of GDP.[61] "More important, if unrecoverable bank loans were included, total debt would already account for more than 45% of GDP."[62]

Such debt/GDP ratios become far more serious when one considers that China's public sector revenue/GDP ratio is only 13 percent, compared to the 30 percent or more ratios typical of many European countries (and of pre-reform China). A deficit of 3 percent is much harder to fund in China than in other countries, because its GDP growth generates far less revenue for the government. "One measure of the repayment ability is the debt dependency ratio of fiscal expenditure, that is, the amount of debt issued divided by the expenditures in the same year. The ratio for the central government budget has exceeded 50 percent since 1994, and was over 70 percent in 1998. This is probably among the highest in the world."[63] Thus there are real limits on how much more the Chinese government can safely increase its deficit spending.

Moreover, the demands on the central budget are growing rapidly as more layoffs take place and new nationally funded pension funds and welfare programs are supposed to replace those that were previously funded and organized by individual state enterprises. Thus the Chinese economy is facing growing structural problems that will not be easily overcome. For example, if the government reduces its spending or seriously tightens money and credit growth, then state enterprises—and even a significant number of non-state enterprises— could easily go under, pushing the economy into a serious recession while adding further to government budget liabilities including the amount of bad loans on the books of the state banks and AMCs.

In addition, because government spending has not solved the problem of overproduction, i.e., of overaccumulation of both money and real capital relative to profitable and productive opportunities for their employment, its longer-term effect has been to fuel a nationwide speculative boom in the real estate sector. Thus, overpriced and largely vacant luxury and semi-luxury housing as well as commercial structures now coexist with excess industrial capacity. As of September 2003, "Some 17% of new bank loans now are related to property, an all-time high."[64] It should be noted that China's last cycle of real estate boom and bust, which ended eight years ago and was much less widespread and intense than the current one, "added huge amounts to banks' bad-loan tallies, so if another bust is big enough, it would have severe implications" not only for the banks but for "affiliated industries like cement and steel, [and] jobs in construction"—not to mention "the specter of a middle class disaffected by a drop in home values."[65]

Facing diminishing benefits from its more traditional policy options, it is not surprising that the reform process has pushed the Chinese government to place greater and greater emphasis on exports and FDI to boost the economy. Proof of the increasing importance of foreign economic activity is easy to find: a 21 percent jump in exports accounted for roughly one-third of China's real GDP growth in 1997; a 38 percent year-on-year rise in exports accounted for roughly four-fifths of real GDP growth in the first half of 2000.[66] According to Stephen Roach, chief economist at Morgan Stanley, although exports made up only approximately 26 percent of the economy in 2002, they accounted for 74 percent of China's economic growth that year. Much of the remaining 26 percent ascribed to domestic demand was indirectly attributable to state spending and FDI.[67]

This growing reliance on exports and FDI helps explain the Chinese government's determined push to join the WTO. But China's accession to the WTO comes at a high cost. In order to get its foot in the WTO door, China was forced to sign a "normal trade relations" (NTR) agreement with the United States. As Eva Cheng notes, the NTR

covers virtually all sectors. A crucial plank is the ending of the state monopoly, within three years, on the importing, distributing and exporting of most goods—industrial, agricultural and transport, even in the sensitive areas of

telecommunications, wholesale, maintenance and repair....In addition, all
restrictions on the quantity of imports will be eliminated progressively within
five years (just two years for U.S. priority products, such as fiber optic
cable)....For all major service categories, restrictions on foreign ownership
have been significantly relaxed (allowing full control in some cases)....For
banks and insurance firms, in particular, imperialist capital's long battle to
secure the right to sell services to the Chinese population (in hitherto sensitive areas such as local currency transactions with Chinese firms and group,
and health and pension, insurance products) is largely won.[68]

The NTR's free-market provisions involve more than foreign investment and trade; they extend deeply into the domestic economic
structure. "China pledged...to allow prices for traded goods and
services in every sector to be determined by market forces, except for
a few products specified in the protocol."[69] The agreement requires
that "SOEs and state investment firms will trade according to commercial principles, and the government will avoid influencing commercial decisions of SOEs."[70] It is no exaggeration to suggest that
the WTO pledges not only "imply the complete and irreversible
destruction of the last remnants of the planned economy and the
complete restoration of capitalism, but also amount to giving up
substantial economic sovereignty to imperialism."[71]

The WTO agreement can only accelerate the negative social trends
and tensions previously highlighted. Ofreneo thus observes that "the
ranks of the rural poor and the floating population are likely to grow":

> To comply with the WTO, China will reduce whatever subsidy it is extending
> to the grain farmers and will increasingly liberalize the importation of grain.
> Already, American and other foreign grain companies are poised to dump
> wheat, corn, and other agricultural products commanding higher prices in
> China. Agriculture is clearly one area where the US expects to gain in trade
> with China under WTO rules (the other main area is in high-tech products).[72]

Workers in state-owned enterprises can also expect to suffer. As a
Hong Kong trade union leader explains:

Attracting foreign investors to invest in or buy-out state enterprises is the ultimate goal. Under deals made to gain entry into the WTO, the Chinese government will lift restrictions on foreign ownership in major sectors over the next 3 to 5 years. This means that officials in charge of major state-owned enterprises are preparing these companies for partnerships with foreign investors, and even takeovers....A key part of this drive to become attractive to foreign investors is the aggressive down-sizing of the workforce and cuts to labor costs. These cuts include removal of all financial obligations to former employees. These cuts, together with widespread corruption among state enterprise managers, has led many state enterprises to violate the terms of agreements given to retrenched workers and the refusal to pay wages, pensions and compensation.[73]

Significantly, even UNCTAD predicts rising unemployment as a result of the opening up of the Chinese economy. UNCTAD expects a surge of imports that directly compete with SOE production, threatening the jobs of many remaining SOE workers. At the same time,

a rapid redeployment of labor to more competitive export-oriented, labor-intensive manufacturing is probably not feasible; nor is it advisable since it could flood the markets in these products and provoke contingency protection measures by China's trading partners through various mechanisms, such as transitional product-specific safeguards which are included among the conditions of accession agreed by China. Although a number of domestic policy instruments may be deployed to defend jobs so as to allow more gradual reform, problems of adjustment can be expected to arise in the short and medium term in sectors dominated by SOEs.[74]

UNCTAD goes on to assess the scale of restructuring as follows:

Removal of subsidies, reduction of tariffs and NTMs [non-tariff measures], and elimination of preferential treatment will, no doubt, exert considerable pressure on these [state-owned] enterprises to improve efficiency and competitiveness, which may call for considerable restructuring and labor-shedding....The scale of restructuring that remains to be done is immense. It has been estimated that about 35 million workers, or 17 percent of the urban work force, are redundant. According to a recent study, China's accession to the WTO could cause unemployment to rise as high as 25 million over the period 2001–2006.[75]

Adding to the employment problem is the fact that recently established foreign operations have become increasingly capital intensive, while inward FDI may even reduce employment insofar as it involves purchases of, or increased competition with, preexisting firms. As Yufan observes:

> More and more FDI is now buying up SOEs and therefore destroying jobs rather than creating them. Even in cases where FDI is for building entirely new plants, it is usually aimed at gaining markets that originally belonged to SOEs, implying that more jobs are going to disappear alongside new jobs created within foreign companies.[76]

Although export-oriented FDI may not have the same job-displacement effects, China cannot hope to boost its more traditional labor-intensive exports sufficiently to provide the needed growth in employment. Indeed, table 9 shows that by 1995, manufacturing employment had already begun to decline, both absolutely and as a percent of total employment, despite continued rapid growth in manufacturing production and exports. The service sector and construction (the latter mainly dependent on government spending and the real estate bubble) have thus been left to take up the growing numbers of workers exiting from agriculture and other rural pursuits. And a huge overhang of over 300 million largely underemployed workers remains in the rural sector.

China's ability to generate jobs for this huge labor surplus is further threatened by the focus of the country's exports on the U.S. market. U.S. action to reduce China's growing trade surplus is looking ever more likely. For example, the U.S. government is pressing China hard to revalue its currency and speed up the opening of its markets to U.S. agricultural products in an attempt to reduce China's large bilateral trade surplus. Besides, it is unlikely that the U.S. trade deficit can continue to grow without limit regardless of the preferred stance of U.S. policy makers on China.

In sum, despite its rapid growth, the Chinese economy is becoming ever more unbalanced and vulnerable to crisis. And, at the same time, living and working conditions for growing numbers of Chinese workers are deteriorating. To this point we have focused on the narrowly defined economic tensions and contradictions generated by the reform process; but insofar as the success of this process in capitalist terms both depends upon and intensifies labor repression and exploitation, it can be expected to generate growing working-class resistance. This could prove to be the most powerful contradiction generated by China's transformation.

RESISTANCE

Chinese workers are often dismissed as a passive mass, incapable of self-organization or collective action. Such a characterization represents a serious misreading of Chinese history. Urban workers engaged in a number of heroic mass strikes during the 1920s and 1930s in support of the revolutionary movement. Workers also engaged in direct actions throughout the Mao era to defend their immediate interests as well as secure greater democratic control over enterprise management. As noted in the previous chapter, in the face of strong party opposition, urban workers struck and employed slowdowns from 1949 to 1952. They renewed their activism in the mid-1950s, culminating in an April–May 1957 strike wave that was influenced by events in Hungary as well as encouraged by Mao's Hundred Flowers Movement. Taking advantage of new freedoms during the Cultural Revolution, workers launched another strike wave in 1967. They also expressed their general frustration with economic, political, and social conditions in 1976, in the events surrounding the April 5 incident.

Given this history, it should not be surprising that workers have, with increasing energy and determination, protested against the negative social consequences of capitalist restoration. A case in point: beginning in 1979, workers sought to use the openings created by the Democracy Wall Movement (1978–81) to express their opposition to Deng's reform process. Relying on methods and strategies learned during the Cultural Revolution, and influenced by the growth of the Solidarity union movement in Poland, they formed unofficial groups and publications to press for the freedom to form independent unions. "Several outbreaks of industrial unrest in China in the early 1980s were reported to have culminated in a demand for free trade unions to be established, including the dispute at the Taiyun Iron and Steel works in 1981."[77]

The following statement from the journal *Sailing Ship*, an unofficial publication of the Taiyuan Iron and Steel workers, illustrates how growing numbers of workers understood their situation in this period:

> They [the workers] understand that if they want to change their wretched conditions, they cannot rely on any messiah, but must begin to organize themselves, to rely on their own strength, and to elect their own representatives to speak for them, and if at any time their elected representatives do not represent them properly, they will be recalled and another election held. This sort of demand on the part of the broad popular masses is the social basis for China's democratic reform.[78]

Deng, who initially supported the Democracy Wall Movement because he found it useful in his own campaign against the Cultural Revolution, soon changed his position and suppressed it by arresting many of its leaders and outlawing its publications when he realized that his own policies were becoming its target. However, as social conditions worsened over the decade, students drew upon the legacy of this movement in launching their own Democracy Movement in 1989.

Students began gathering in Tiananmen Square in April to demand political reform. As demonstrations and crowds grew in size over the following weeks, more and more working people became involved. A core group of workers were inspired to form the Beijing Autonomous Workers' Federation. The federation grew quickly to a membership of between 10,000 and 20,000, although that number was more a reflection of political support for worker rights then a measure of organized strength in the workplace. As interest in the Democracy Movement spread to other cities during May, new Autonomous Worker Federations (WAFs) were formed and networked together.

On June 2, the official Chinese union federation called for the banning of the WAFs as illegal organizations. Two days later, the government took forcible action to end the democracy movement. Workers involved with the WAFs were especially targeted for punishment.

There were several new attempts at independent labor organizing in the early 1990s. The Free Trade Unions of China was formed in Beijing in 1991. In 1994, the League for the Protection of the Rights of Working People was established in Beijing. That same year, the Hired-Hand Workers Federation was formed in Shenzhen. Each of these groups was small and did not last long in the face of government repression. However, they represented a significant movement forward from the WAFs in that these initiatives were more directly concerned with worker organizing.[79]

While arrests of labor activists succeeded in crushing efforts to build independent working class organizations in the 1990s, it did not stop the steady and accelerating growth of labor activism. In the early years of reform, working-class resistance was mostly limited to the special export processing zone on the east coast, where courageous (and largely female-led) workers engaged in wildcat strikes, slowdowns, and individual acts of sabotage to protest exploitative work conditions, especially in factories run by foreign capital.[80] Subsequently, labor protest has broadened to encompass laid-off SOE workers, workers in privatized enterprises subject to wage and benefit cuts and speed-ups, and farmers and other rural poor.

Even facing "ferocious state repression of labor activists," Chinese workers nationwide have engaged in public protests demanding that their right to subsistence be protected.[81] On December 24, 1997, the *New York Times* relayed "numerous reports of small-scale worker protests around the country over such concerns as nonpayment of wages or pensions, fear of job losses after corporate takeovers, and conflicts over dismissals and severance pay."[82] Two days later, the Associated Press observed:

> Sacrificed to save decrepit state industries, the jobless are looking for work by the millions across China—an army of the discontented that has jolted the communist government with a spreading wave of protests....So far the protests have remained small and centered on local issues....Demonstrations have bedeviled China all year—more than 450 in the first six months alone, according to exiled labor activist Han Dongfang. Much of the unrest...has taken place in Sichuan, a landlocked province saddled with outmoded factories far from prosperous

coastal markets. But in the past few weeks, protests have spread to the eastern
city of Hefei and to the coal-mining town of Jiaohe in the northeast.[83]

The *Los Angeles Times* summed up the situation as of spring 1999:

> Reports are rife of labor unrest across the country, from Hunan province in the
> south to here in the northeast, China's rust belt...(T)he government fears that
> laborers—particularly the unemployed, who number between 15 million and
> 25 million in China—might organize en masse to become the wellspring of
> new opposition to Communist rule. Or, worse yet, that disgruntled workers
> might try to link up with other disenfranchised groups, such as political dissi-
> dents, to create some sort of united national front.[84]

Official Chinese statistics confirm the reports of growing labor
resistance. There were 198,000 officially reported labor disputes in
1999. That number rose to 327,152 in 2000. As Pringle notes, "These
statistics represent the continuation of a spectacular increase in disputes that began in the early 1990s."[85] These labor dispute statistics
include individual labor disputes that are often settled through
China's legal system, as well as more significant collective actions.
Looking just at the latter, which normally require and/or produce
greater organization, unity, and class consciousness, we find a similar trend. There were 6,767 collective actions (usually strikes or
slowdowns involving a minimum of three workers) involving
251,268 people in 1998. This represented an increase in collective
actions of 900 percent from 1992. In 2000, the official total of collective actions grew to 8,247, involving 259,445 workers.[86]

A new and even more significant wave of labor activism began in
spring 2002. According to one analyst, its significance lies in the fact
that it involved "stronger membership, unity, leadership, and a better
level of organization."[87] From March to May some 80,000 workers in
two northeastern provinces engaged in unprecedented demonstrations that lasted for months. Approximately 50,000 oil workers
marched and demonstrated in Daqing City in Heilongjiang province;
more than 30,000 workers from more than 20 state-owned enterprises held demonstrations in Liaoyang City in Liaoning province. "In

both cases workers were demanding unpaid wages, pension and compensation, as well as protesting against the corruption and injustice of local officials and enterprise managers. And in both cases police and armed soldiers were deployed to put down the protests."[88]

The Daqing worker protests included the formation of an independent labor organization, the Daqing Provisional Union of Retrenched Workers, which included a large number of workers from the same workplace. Equally significant, despite government efforts to isolate the workers, news of their actions spread beyond Heilongjiang province, leading oil workers in other provinces to stage solidarity strikes and protests.[89]

The Laioyang protest by workers at the Ferroalloy Factory began as a relatively small action involving only a few thousand workers, but grew stronger and larger in response to state repression. As Trini Leung explains:

> Police brutality against the demonstrations and the detention of several representatives one week after the first protest action was staged brought 30,000 workers from over a dozen factories out in the streets of Liaoyang to express their support and solidarity for the Ferroalloy workers. The Ferroalloy workers continued for several months to organize regular demonstrations demanding the government release their representatives and respond to their calls for investigation into corruption in their enterprise and in the local government. The main strength of the Liaoyang protests lies in their high level of organization which unites the plant's workers around an open leadership. In this sense the Liaoyang Ferroalloy Factory workers have organized the most successful archetype of an independent union in China since 1949.[90]

Meanwhile, in rural areas, "The peasant class, whose dissatisfaction has driven governments from power throughout China's history, is growing restive again, swelling the ranks of the country's disaffected along with laid-off workers, struggling pensioners and the millions of Chinese who have migrated from the countryside to cities where they eke out a tenuous existence."[91] Farmers are protesting low agricultural prices, high taxes and administrative fees (used largely to finance the luxurious lifestyles of the party elite), and the police practice of meting out beatings to those who cannot afford to pay taxes.[92] Perhaps the most notable protest by farmers took place in August 2000, in Yuandu, Jiangxi province (in south-central China):

> More than 10,000 angry peasants converged on the two-story, white-tiled town hall here in August, demanding relief from high taxes and administrative fees that eat up any profit from farming....According to residents, terrified town officials barricaded themselves inside the building on Aug. 17 before 30 truckloads of armed police arrived to disperse the crowd. At least one farmer was severely beaten in the ensuing melee, and more than a dozen others were carted away....When word of the Yuandu protest spread, thousands more angry farmers rampaged through neighboring towns...breaking windows and even attacking the homes of some officials. Farmers say the police are still searching for leaders of the protests.[93]

The overall impression given by the Chinese working-class movement is one of spontaneous, decentralized, and uncoordinated resistance—but not completely so. When thousands of laid-off workers in Mianyang, Sichuan province, conducted a street demonstration on July 7, 1997, "to demand new jobs," exiled labor activists described the action as an outgrowth of protests that had been going on for many months, "involving as many as 100,000 people in all."[94] The protest wave apparently included "not only workers, but also peasants...working in close co-operation," and "staging sit-ins and marches" for at least a year. "Job losses have not been the only issue: the elderly have been demanding overdue pension payments, and peasants have been calling for compensation for land taken over by the government."[95]

Even smaller individual upsurges have been partly preplanned. When an August 1997 demonstration by 20 laid-off workers outside city offices in Dujiangyan, southwestern China, was attacked by the police (who struck and kicked the protesters), workers were enraged. They responded by organizing "days of larger, noisier protests," receiving the support of "pedicab drivers," who, "as word of the confrontation spread...came out in force over the next few days to tie up traffic."[96]

Perhaps the most striking example of organized action involves the Daqing workers. "There have been reports that preparations for [the Daqing Provisional Union of Retrenched Workers] had been taking place quite some time before the March actions, indicating that the action was not spontaneous....The high level of organization and the relatively long period of preparation for the outbreak of protest actions is illustrated by the [fact that] the provisional union issued notices signed by its leaders."[97]

To this point the government has been largely successful in containing worker protests and isolating and repressing activists. As Sophie Beach observes:

> Without independent unions or peasant associations to protect their interests, workers and villagers regularly stage public protests against corruption, unemployment and economic disparities that allow the rich to get richer while the poor frequently can't even get their paychecks. But when protesters point out the sources of their problems and demand democracy and legal protection of their rights, authorities are quick to crack down.[98]

Indeed, China's increasingly bourgeois state has registered its concern with growing worker militancy by bolstering its judicial and coercive means of repression. In November 1999, the government "announced new rules for public gatherings, requiring assemblies larger than 200 to obtain approval from local public security authorities. Gatherings larger than 3000 will require the approval of security offices at a higher level."[99] Although ostensibly targeting new spiritual movements such as the Falun Gong group, there was no doubt that the new rules would be applied to worker-community protests. Indeed, "while few Western commentators seem to remember, the Communist regime is acutely aware that economic and labor grievances played an important role in the 1989 protests"; hence "the prospect of labor unrest worries China's Communist leaders the most."[100] The central government continues to arrest anyone who tries to form an independent labor organization, and just to make its intentions clear it "ordered cities across the country to augment their anti-riot police" in January 2001.[101]

CONCLUSION

As we have seen, China's economic reforms have generated serious economic imbalances as well as industrial growth. They have also largely destroyed the framework and institutional capacity necessary for creating a nationally integrated and responsive political economy.

Growing numbers of Chinese working people have paid a high price for their country's capitalist transformation, and many are beginning to demonstrate their determination and ability to defend their interests. The government's success in containing worker protests to this point does not change the fact that the ongoing capitalization of China's economy is likely to bring further deterioration of living and working conditions for many Chinese workers. Thus, new and perhaps even more organized opposition to state policies can be expected, with potentially serious implications for China's export-oriented, foreign-dependent economy.[102]

It remains for progressives to decide how they want to relate to present and future working-class activism in China. However, insofar as they continue to celebrate China as a "socialist" or even progressive development success story, they will find themselves taking an increasingly reactionary position vis-à-vis both Chinese politics and worker-community struggles. As the Chinese experience makes clear, there has never been a greater need to strengthen the class-based critique of markets and market socialism, and return to a vision of socialism based on the power of the associated producers.

4

Contradictions of China's
Transformation: International

China has become a major regional and global economic force. It has not only recorded double-digit real GDP growth for most of the decade 1985–95, but also maintained rapid growth of over 7 percent per year during and after the 1997–98 East Asian crisis. According to Stephen Roach, chief economist for Morgan Stanley, "China's growth rate is now strong enough to have accounted for 17.5 percent of the growth in world gross domestic product [in 2002]—second only to the growth contribution of the United States."[1] By 2002, China's shares of Asian GDP and exports stood at over 17 percent and 20 percent, respectively.[2] Some purchasing power estimates have China accounting for half of Asia's GDP.[3]

Many progressive scholars and activists, mesmerized by the country's rapid export-led growth, have declared China to be an economic success. Even more important, they have promoted China as a development model whose growth strategy can and should be emulated by other countries. We have argued, based on an analysis of China's domestic economic dynamics, that this is a serious mistake, one that reflects a misunderstanding of the Chinese experience. In this chapter we reinforce our argument by showing how this embrace of "China as model" also reflects a misunderstanding of the contradictory logic of capitalism as an international system.

In fact, as we shall see, the nature and consequences of China's rapid economic transformation cannot be fully grasped in isolation from the broader dynamics of global capitalism, especially uneven development and overproduction. Our analysis of these dynamics highlights the ways in which China's economic growth has been enabled by, and in turn accentuated, the contradictions of capitalist development in other countries. In other words, China's growth both reflects, and contributes to, capitalism's limitation of development possibilities around the world. Thus, rather than offering a model of development that deserves our support, China's growth strategy only heightens competitive pressures throughout the region to the detriment of workers and their communities.

REGIONAL CONTRADICTIONS OF CHINA'S TRANSFORMATION

As previously noted, China's growing regional economic dominance is due largely to its success in attracting FDI. As table 10 shows, net FDI flows into China have dwarfed those obtained by neighboring countries for the years 1997–2002. Indeed, except for China and Hong Kong, and a temporary uptick associated with post-crisis "vulture investments" in Thailand and South Korea, net FDI in the major East Asian economies either stagnated or was actually negative in the years following the 1997–98 crisis. As a result of these FDI trends, China is becoming the major export center in the region (excluding Japan).

Table 11 indicates that, apart from Indonesia (a significant oil exporter), China is the only country whose exports did not decrease in 2001, in response to recessions in external core markets, especially the United States. Notice also that the grand total of exports of the major East Asian economies has grown much more slowly since 1995 than previously, when the tendency was for exports to double every five years. In short, China is taking up a rising share of an increasingly stagnant total of regional exports.

Not only is China coming to dominate the region's exports, it is moving rapidly to transform the nature of its own exports. For example, in 1985, 49 percent of its exports were of primary products and resource-based manufactures. In 2000, the export share of these products had fallen to approximately 12 percent, with nonresource-based manufactures accounting for approximately 88 percent. The share of high-technology exports jumped from 3 percent to 22 percent over the same period.[4]

The rapid rise of China as a major exporter of electronics is highlighted by the results of a 2003 study by the Japan Electronic and Information Technology Industries Association. According to the study, China will be the largest electronics exporter in the world in 2003 with the highest market share in 8 out of 12 major export items. These include mobile phones, color TV sets, laptop computers, desktop PCs, PDAs (Personal Digital Assistants), DVD players, DVD drives, and car stereos. This represents a steady climb for China. It was number one in only two categories in 2000, three in 2001, and five in 2002. "Among the four items not dominated by China, Japan is expected to lead in digital cameras, and car navigators, Indonesia in VTRs [Video Tape Recorders], and Singapore in HDDs [Hard Disk Drives], respectively. However, China is likely to catch up with Indonesia and Singapore within two years as production of VTRs and HDDs is showing rapid growth."[5]

This transformation in exports has of course been powered by foreign companies, as Stephen Roach points out:

> For more than a decade, the vigor of Chinese export growth has come far more from the deliberate outsourcing strategies of western multinational companies than from the rapid growth of indigenous Chinese companies. From 1994 to mid-2003, China's exports tripled from $121 bn to $365 bn. It turns out that "foreign-invested enterprises"—Chinese subsidiaries of global multinationals and joint ventures with businesses from the industrialized world—account for fully 65 percent of the total increase in Chinese exports over that period.[6]

The dominance of foreign firms in China's high-tech exports is illustrative. In 1996, foreign affiliates accounted for 59 percent of these exports. They accounted for 74 percent in 1998, and 81 percent in 2000.[7]

Because of this transformation in exports, China now represents a very serious threat to the continued viability of the region's other export-led economies. For example, according to the Philippine economist Rene Ofreneo:

> Today, even the more developed Asian economies such as Singapore are now feeling the pinch of competition by a fully awakened Chinese dragon, as the latter is slowly succeeding in developing depth and quality in industrial structure. Aside from low-priced labor-intensive products such as baby dresses, China is now producing more and more low-priced medium-tech products such as electrical appliances like televisions, washing machines, photocopiers, and electronic products such as computer peripherals, keyboards, disc drives, and desktop personal computers. Thus, for almost all the Southeast Asian economies, China is now seen as a competitor.[8]

The Bank for International Settlements offers a similar perspective:

> China is already a major producer of labor-intensive manufactures. Moreover, as a result of its accession to the WTO, it is expected to capture a large share of the liberalized global market in textiles and apparel when the WTO Agreement on Textiles and Clothing expires in 2005. China thus poses major challenges for current producers of textiles and other labor intensive manufactures in Southeast Asia. In addition, the country has moved steadily up the value added chain, and its exports of machinery and high-tech products have increased rapidly. China's share in Asia's total electronics exports has more than doubled during the past five years to 30% in 2002. In contrast, the shares of Malaysia and Singapore have fallen off sharply. Anecdotal accounts also suggest that production facilities in high-tech sectors are being relocated to China from emerging East Asia as well as Japan.[9]

The overarching explanation for China's regional dominance is that it has become the most attractive platform for East Asia's export assault on the U.S. market. Foreign firms operating in China "run a trade surplus primarily with the United States and deficits with the East and Southeast Asian economies. This suggests that FDI from investors in East Asia uses China as an export platform for the Western markets, and that their home countries provide the inputs needed in such operations."[10]

Table 12 highlights this development, revealing China's increasing overall share of the region's exports to the United States. Here again, the tendency is for China to take up a growing share of a more slowly growing regional export total. Table 13 shows that the rising share of China's exports destined for the United States has corresponded to a somewhat reduced reliance on the U.S. market by most of the other major East Asian exporters. Table 14 provides a broader perspective on the same shifts. Generally speaking, the declining share of China's exports to Asia compared to extra-regional core markets finds its mirror image in the trends for other East Asian countries.

While progressive supporters of China have tended to sidestep the question of whether China's growth represents a threat to the economic health of other countries in the region, neoliberal analysts have generally been more forthright. Most have argued that despite the FDI and export trends highlighted above, China's rise actually represents an opportunity rather than a threat for the other economies in the region. After all, they claim, this is not the first time that the region has had a significant restructuring of production relations, and earlier restructuring episodes ushered in the now legendary growth miracles of Japan, the four "little tigers" (South Korea, Taiwan, Singapore, and Hong Kong), and the most recent export-led growth miracles of the so-called ASEAN [Association of Southeast Asian Nations]-3—Malaysia, Indonesia, and Thailand.

Indeed, it is argued that the large absolute size of the Chinese economy and the fact that China's exports are import dependent make China's growth an increasingly powerful regional economic locomotive. Realization of this potential requires only that East Asian countries respond to the new opportunities by restructuring their own production activity accordingly. This means removing all barriers to the free movement of money, commodity, and productive capital among the region's countries (and similarly deregulating the internal workings of each country's economy) so that transnational capital can establish a more "efficient," i.e., profit maximizing, regional division of labor. Only if the different countries of the region fail to do this will China pose a threat rather than an opportunity.

Along these lines, Ramkishen Rajan dismisses the "growing fears that Southeast Asia is 'losing out' in the intense competition for FDI inflows to China," together with the "export pessimism that has been voiced by a number of regional observers and policy makers," as simple "fallacies of composition":

> To be sure, with the major improvements in transportation, coordination and communication technologies, globalization provides vastly increased opportunities for the fragmentation of previously integrated goods and services into their constituent [productive activities] which in turn may be spread across counties on the basis of comparative advantage. The importance of such "production sharing" is that it suggests that openness, by expanding opportunities for international specialization and trade, will be beneficial to all parties involved....Seen through the lense of production-sharing, the cost effectiveness of the PRC ought to benefit all countries that are part of the production network.[11]

Similarly, in arguing that China's "emergence...presents as many opportunities as threats to East Asian policy makers," Asian Development Bank economist David Roland-Holst forecasts that China's "long-term trajectory will make it a prominent importer in East Asia" as well as a formidable export competitor.[12] For "individual East Asian economies," China's growing regional and global economic presence requires that "they adapt to more open multilateralism, regionally or globally joining efforts to reduce barriers to trade. Only in this way can they avoid crowding out from their established export markets and fully capture new export opportunities...represented mainly by PRC, directly in terms of its burgeoning domestic demand, and indirectly as it absorbs intermediate goods to meet export demand from the Rest of the World."[13]

The potential developmental synergies from the combination of China's emergence and regional integration form the basis of neoliberal optimism about the prospective incorporation of China into the ASEAN Free Trade Area (AFTA) by 2010, for which an agreement in principle was reached at the November 2002 ASEAN meetings. The resulting ASEAN-China Free Trade Area (ACFTA) will, according to

Thai economist Suthiphand Chirathivat, "lower costs, increase intra-regional trade and increase economic efficiency," which will in turn "boost real income in both regions as resources flow to sectors where they can be more efficiently and productively utilized."[14] Another Thai economist employed by the ASEAN Secretariat appeals to "the well-known flying geese pattern of collective development" to argue that the ACFTA will yield "good commercial returns in support of income growth, structural transformation and modernization, poverty alleviation, and social advancement across the region":

> The pattern itself is conditioned and facilitated: firstly, by the mutual liberalization of trade and investment, and the associated standardization and simplification of procedures and regulations,...secondly, by the mutual transformation, diversification, and upgrading of sectors, industries, and enterprises among the independent economies and enterprises concerned; thirdly, by the collaborative establishment and deepening of various cross-border linkages and inter-firm partnering; and lastly, by the formation of a common position in commercial diplomacy and in negotiating fora within and outside the region.[15]

However, such neoliberal "win-win" scenarios are far too rosy for several reasons. Most generally, they bypass the class dimension of capitalist development as well as the inherently uneven and unequal development of the global division of labor insofar as it is shaped by the needs of competing transnational capitals. As a result, neoliberal perspectives ignore that the previous growth miracles and economic restructurings occurring in East Asia (starting with Japan in the 1950s) were themselves fraught with instability and crises, were hardly pure positive-sum developments from the standpoint of the regional and world economies as a whole, and came at an extremely high cost for working people even in the "miracle" countries themselves.[16]

More specifically, the connection between the development impasses faced by East and Southeast Asian countries and their ongoing dependence on FDI and exports (this is after all the key reason why China poses such a threat to them) is left unaddressed. Indeed, the suggested adjustment to China's new role in transnational capitalist production chains implies that the region's economies will become even more FDI- and export-oriented. Given that the 1997–98 regional crisis was due in large measure to regional overproduction of exports and the drying up of FDI inflows (and the accompanying cycle of speculative finance) this development can only further unbalance the region's economies.[17]

In this connection, neoliberals fail to give adequate weight to the dangers involved in the region's ever increasing dependence on external markets, highlighted by the size of the U.S. trade deficit and growing imbalances in the U.S. economy, as well as ongoing stagnation in Europe. Equally problematic, the neoliberal scenario sees the region's growth prospects being tied more closely to the health and stability of a China-based export system directed at the United States. However, the health and stability of the Chinese economy is increasingly being threatened by ever larger fiscal deficits and financial imbalances, deflation, and rising social costs and resistance.[18]

Moreover, the neoliberal "win-win" scenario simply assumes that the countries of the region all have the capability to restructure their industries in line with the dictates of transnational capital or, what amounts to the same thing, relegates those unable or unwilling to have their policies dictated in this way to the list of development "failures" to be contrasted with the ever-changing (and, it seems, evershortening) list of neoliberal poster countries. It also ignores (or simply takes as an inevitable fact of life to which "there is no alternative") that attempts to re-attract FDI in the face of competition from China can only mean new state efforts to intensify the exploitation of workers and the environment.

NATIONAL EXPERIENCES

In what follows we examine the likely effects of China's new role on some of East Asia's main economies. This examination makes clear that the foreign-driven rise of China as an export powerhouse will only intensify economic tensions and contradictions throughout the region, to the detriment of workers everywhere. This reality offers yet additional powerful evidence of why China should not be thought of as offering a model of development deserving our support. Said differently, China's rise cannot be understood in isolation from its negative effect on other countries in the region and the world. To celebrate China, to see its strategy as a model, is therefore to be blinded to the uneven and combined process of development that marks capitalism as a world system.

SOUTHEAST ASIA

China's rise is probably most threatening to the ASEAN-4, which includes Indonesia, Thailand, Malaysia, and Singapore. While China's export growth pulls in inputs from throughout the region, including from these countries, the resulting gains can be expected to be of limited value in terms of relaunching these countries onto a new growth trajectory. There are two main reasons for this: first, their exports to China are concentrated in only a few product lines, which in many cases will not contribute to any broad-based industrialization program. Second, these export gains will be far outweighed by losses in existing export markets due to China's own export production.[19] As a result, their forced restructuring will likely lead to a further industrial narrowing and disarticulation, with profoundly negative effects for their respective workers.

Most analysts agree that China's changing export profile represents a serious threat to the future export competitiveness of most Southeast Asian countries. According to Chia Siow Yue, senior research fellow at the Singapore Institute of International Affairs, the export overlap between China and Indonesia is 83 percent and the overlap between China and Singapore is 38 percent.[20] The World Bank takes much the same position: "The correlation of exports, even at the five-digit (SITC) level between China and middle-income countries such as Indonesia and Thailand is significant and has been increasing."[21] This threat to Indonesian and Thai exports

is confirmed by a market-by-market and product-by-product analysis for sample countries. For this analysis we identify "exports at risk" to the U.S. and Japan markets based on their importance to the exporting country and the extent to which they compete with similar products from China. Exports in product categories that are characterized by both a high share of Chinese imports (at least 5 percent) and unit values close to those of competing imports from China are deemed to be most at risk. For Thailand and Indonesia, the results show that 15–25 percent of exports to the United States and Japan are at risk from growing competition from China.[22]

The garment and textile industries are especially at risk. Malaysia, Thailand, Indonesia, and the Philippines are all expected to lose market share in the U.S. and West European markets when quotas on Chinese textiles and apparel exports are lifted. One estimate is that China's exports of apparel can be expected to grow by 330 percent over a ten year period now that it is a member of the WTO. China's share would then be over 44 percent of the world total.[23]

China's growth is pulling in imports from these countries, but these imports cannot easily compensate for their loss of export markets. In the case of Indonesia, for example, its exports to China are heavily concentrated in primary commodities such as processed oil, rubber, palm and timber. The World Bank, ever optimistic, argues that Indonesia can, if it liberalizes its economy, take advantage of new opportunities structured by China's ongoing economic transformation to ensure the further development of its own industrial sector. For example:

Opportunities exist for Indonesia to participate in global production networks—cosmetics, machinery, and audiovisual equipment, for example—in which FDI may expand in China and Indonesia simultaneously. And, like other ASEAN middle-income countries, Indonesia has the potential to develop its role as a supplier of specific parts to an automobile production network, given the restructuring of the industry now taking place in the region….Indonesia will need to tailor its strategy to grasp the opportunities for increases in trade and investment flows if it is to offset the declines that are projected in its exports to the United States, Japan, and the EU. Key elements will be measures to restore investor confidence and increase competitiveness. Indonesia will need to avoid protecting its domestic producers with excessive safeguard measures so as to facilitate an adjustment in the manufacturing sector that responds to the opportunities in China's markets.

Measures like the recently introduced temporary safeguards against garment imports, for example, will only prolong the adjustments that Indonesia needs to make to realize its regional comparative advantages.[24]

However, based on existing trends, it seems doubtful that Indonesia will attract the foreign investment it needs to achieve the recommended product specialization. "Foreign investment approvals for the first nine months of the year [2003] totaled just $6.1 billion, a 3.7% increase over the same period in 2002 but a far cry from pre-crisis levels in the mid-1990s."[25] Indeed, with "parts of the labor-intensive manufacturing sector...relocating to lower-cost competitors like Vietnam and China," *net* FDI inflows have become increasingly negative (see table 10).[26]

Broadly speaking, Thailand's economic situation is similar to Indonesia's. Its trade opportunities with China are heavily oriented toward agricultural products such as oilseeds, sugar, wood products and cotton. And as its manufactures get squeezed out of third markets, it will be forced to adjust its industrial structure if it wants to sustain its manufacturing base. The World Bank's advice is accordingly as follows:

> The extent to which Thailand will exit from assembly-type production or upgrade its capabilities will depend largely on the policies it pursues—either embracing trade-induced competitiveness and productivity gains, or submitting to short-term protectionist pressures; manufacturers already are complaining about low-cost imports of electrical appliances and motorbikes from China. Also important are supply factors, including local availability of engineering and sourcing capabilities, as are government incentives for upgrading technology.[27]

Again, the World Bank advocates for a further deregulation and denationalization of the economy, in the belief that new foreign initiatives can produce the desired restructuring. This strategy would, of course, tie Thailand ever more tightly into a foreign-dominated export-led growth strategy with China as a geographical focal point.

The Malaysian economy is more developed than those of Indonesia and Thailand, but it also faces a serious challenge. Malaysia's export profile has already shifted from textiles and apparel to the electrical machinery sector, so China's predicted growth in textiles and apparel is not so damaging. Electrical machinery exports grew from 9.9 percent of Malaysia's exports in 1980, to 26.6 percent in 1990, and 33.6 percent in 1996. But, the share of electrical machinery exports in China's trade almost doubled over the period 1990–96, to 12.3 percent. Its share has grown substantially since then.[28]

Thus, China's continuing export transformation now threatens one of Malaysia's leading export sectors. Although the disappearance of 16,000 jobs from the country's electronics production hub in Penang state in 2001 was partly due to the U.S. recession, the fact is that "new investment has dwindled as companies expand in China instead."[29] Referring to the 39 percent (seasonally adjusted) decline in Malaysia's electronics exports in the third quarter of 2003 (following a 14.5 percent drop in the previous quarter), the *Far Eastern Economic Review* observes: "The numbers confirm one disturbing fact: The relocation of electronics companies, which produce personal computers, cell phones and routers, from Malaysia to more cost-competitive production centers, particularly China, is starting to take its toll."[30]

Of particular concern is the possible loss of Japanese electronics FDI, which has been crucial to the development of Malaysia's exporting capabilities. As one regional analyst summarizes the situation:

> For the computer and electronics sub-sector that constitute the major manufacture export of Malaysia, the labor-intensive portion of this product group will also be affected negatively. On the other hand, the future of high technology exports from Malaysia that utilize skilled labor will depend on the future of foreign direct investment, given the dependency for FDI in this sub-sector....In 1998, based on companies in production, Japanese Direct Investment (JDI) in Malaysia in the electrical and electronics sub-sectors amounted to RM 4408 million and accounted for 57 percent of total JDI in this country. In contrast, American FDI in the same sub-sector for the same year in Malaysia amounted to only RM 770 million and accounted for 35 percent of total American FDI in this country. FDI from Japan comprised of 56 percent total foreign investment in the electrical and electronics sub-sector in 1998 while the United States is the third largest investor with a share of 9.8

percent. Consequently the future of high technology exports depends on the future of JDI in this sub-sector.[31]

More broadly, it was Japanese-led regional FDI that helped to promote the rapid growth and industrialization not only of Malaysia but also of Thailand and Indonesia. Japanese firms now appear determined to reorient their regional production base toward China. This shift means that the underlying framework for the Southeast Asian growth strategies has been gravely weakened if not shattered. Although neoliberals argue that the ASEAN countries can counter this problem by technologically upgrading their production into higher value-added products, China itself "is now starting to sell more sophisticated goods to American consumers, like computers and DVDs."[32]

> The intensifying competition from China is even being felt by technologically sophisticated Singapore. In fact, among ASEAN countries, Singapore was hardest hit by the rise of China as an export powerhouse. A report by J. P. Morgan cites the electronics industry as the sector where Singapore suffered the most, despite it being a higher value-added producer than China. "As electronics firms relocated to China and established clusters in North Asia," it says, "Singapore's regional status in the electronics chain was eroded." In other words just having a more sophisticated production base does not guarantee security. From 1997 to 2002, China's share of Asia's electronics exports (excluding Japan) rose from 14.3 to 30.1 percent. While most countries, including Thailand and Malaysia, suffered small declines, Singapore's share fell substantially from 19.3 to 9.8 percent.[33]

Given the presumed absence of any alternative to development through participation in transnational capitalist production chains, one can understand the increasingly desperate efforts of the ASEAN countries to accelerate their economic integration in order to attract the FDI needed to reinvigorate exports and growth. Hence, in the run-up to the October 2003 ASEAN meetings, all the talk concerned how, "facing competition from China...Asean is being forced to confront its failure to realize a long-held goal: integration into a single market that is attractive to foreign investors."[34]

The sudden urgency to accept the PRC's offer to establish an ASEAN-China Free Trade Area should be seen in this light. While Rajan argues that "an immediate...side effect of the ACFTA proposal is that it appears to have provided an impetus for Southeast Asian countries to hasten the process of intra-ASEAN integration," the converse is undoubtedly also true.[35]

In contrast to the optimistic notions of neoliberal industrial restructuring theorists, some analysts argue that the ASEAN countries should just accept the reality of China's dominance in manufacturing and focus their development efforts on natural resources and tourism. "'That's a more realistic option, if you ask me, than to keep saying we are going to compete with China in manufacturing at the high end, because China is moving fast into the high end as well,' said Toh Kin Woon, the Penang state executive councilor for economic planning."[36] Similarly, after surveying China's competitive threat across the industries that drove the ASEAN growth "miracles," two economists from the National University of Singapore suggest:

> China's emergence as a global manufacturing center has apparently resulted in most ASEAN economies experiencing a severe hollowing-out of their industries....[This] underscores the need for ASEAN to accelerate structural domestic reform and will compel ASEAN economies to base their future economic growth on their true comparative advantage. To meet the challenges posed by China, ASEAN countries will need to specialize in what they produce and develop strengths and core competencies in agriculture, natural resources and services such as tourism.[37]

The developmental limitations of the resource/tourism strategy are painfully obvious, however. For example:

> Daniel Lian, an economist with Morgan Stanley in Singapore, has his doubts. In 2002, manufactured exports from Malaysia, Singapore, Thailand, Indonesia and the Philippines accounted for 54 percent of the five countries' combined gross domestic product of $566 billion....Lian estimates that $90 billion of these exports, or 30 percent of the total, will be lost to China within a decade, while annual receipts from a Chinese-fueled tourism boom cannot

realistically exceed $20 billion to $25 billion...."Tourism cannot replace manufacturing," he said in a report.[38]

In sum, it is hard to see how China's new role in the regional economy can possibly support a positive process of economic development for Southeast Asian countries. Growth will remain export oriented and foreign dependent. And it will be shaped ever more strongly by regional and international forces that are further removed from, and less likely to transfer any lasting benefits to, the workers of these countries. In fact, given their desperation to remain attractive to foreign investment, one can expect that the above highlighted Southeast Asian governments will continue to sacrifice the living and working conditions of their respective workers on the altar of competitiveness.

SOUTH KOREA

South Korea has a far more established and nationally rooted industrial base than the ASEAN countries examined above. And, most mainstream analysts see South Korea as a major beneficiary of China's new growth strategy. Indeed, South Korea has been very aggressive in tapping the China market. "According to a report by the Korea Trade-Investment Promotion Agency, which compared the advancement of Korea, Taiwan and Japan into the Chinese market, Korea's exports in the last 10 years [from 1992 to 2002] grew 530 percent, compared to Taiwan's 290 percent and Japan's 230 percent."[39] As a result, South Korea increased its market share from 5.16 percent of China's imports to 9.68 percent.[40]

In 2002, China became South Korea's largest trading partner in Asia, replacing Japan. China is close to replacing the United States as South Korea's number one export market. Moreover, South Korea has run a trade surplus with China every year since 1992. China has also become the number one location for South Korean FDI, accounting for 40 percent of South Korea's outward FDI as of the first quarter of 2003, compared with 28 percent for the United States.[41]

However, this growing connection to China has a serious downside for the long-term health of the South Korean economy, which has, in fact, been struggling. One important reason is that the FDI that provided needed foreign exchange after the 1997–98 crisis has largely dried up. FDI inflows fell from $15.2 billion in 2000, to $9.1 billion in 2002, and further to $2.7 billion in the first half of 2003.[42] To a large extent this decline is the result of two factors. First, foreign investors took advantage of the South Korean crisis to buy up South Korean assets, and are now largely finished doing that. Second, China presents a more attractive location for new FDI than does South Korea.

Desperate to reverse this downward trend, the South Korean government is proposing special FDI incentives that will lead not only to the further fragmentation and foreign domination of the South Korean economy, but to repression of worker rights. For example, the government has asked the National Assembly to approve the creation of several special economic zones to make South Korea the "business hub of East Asia." Foreign businesses that operate within these zones would enjoy tax breaks as well as exemptions from various environmental and labor regulations. Foreign enterprises would also be given the sole authority to build and operate educational and health institutions, which could serve not only the foreign residents of the zones but also South Koreans. In addition, the government is prepared to offer foreign high-tech investors a cash grant equal to 20 percent of the value of their total investment.[43]

A member of the president's planning commission noted that "Britain, Ireland and China, for instance, are offering generous cash grants to foreign investors, with the specific ratio determined by a detailed analysis of the investment plan." For these reasons, he added, "The Korean government is also planning to adopt a similar incentive system for foreign investors, particularly in the fields of state-of-the-art technologies."[44]

But South Korea is not only losing its battle to attract FDI, it is also facing a major capital flight by South Korean firms. As the *Korea Herald* explains:

> Korean industries are moving overseas faster than firms in other advanced economies, and the so-called industrial hollowing out will likely become a serious problem by 2007, Korea's leading business organization argued yester-

day....According to a report by the Federation of Korean Industries, a lobby group for the nation's business conglomerates, or chaebol, the balance of Korea's overseas direct investment accounted for 5.8 percent of its nominal gross domestic product as of the end of 2000, reaching almost the same level of Japan, whose gross national income per capita was four times as high as that of Korea....If the trend of industrial emigration continues, the ratio of the balance of Korea's overseas direct investment to gross domestic output will rise to 9.7 percent in 2007, and the percentage of manufacturing of total GDP will fall sharply, raising serious concerns about industrial hollowing out, the organization argued....Industrial migration, which in the past took place mostly in light industries such as shoemaking and apparel industries, is rapidly spreading to other sectors, including the electronics, telecommunications, metal and machinery industries, it noted.[45]

South Korean business leaders argue that they are being driven to leave by the high cost and combative nature of workers in South Korea. They are demanding that the South Korean government take action to weaken unions and support their efforts to lower wages and working conditions.[46] And, they claim that if the government does not meet their demands they will continue to move their production "across the Yellow Sea to China, where wages are lower and the demands of workers rarely result in headaches for managers."[47]

This is no idle threat. For example, Samsung Electronics, LG Electronics, and Daewoo Electronics already make more than half of their consumer durables in factories outside of Korea, many of which are in China.[48] Samsung Electronics announced in September 2003 that it was moving its entire PC-making business to China.[49]

This shift in production to China may well enhance the profitability of South Korean multinational corporations. It is unlikely, however, to strengthen the South Korean economy. It will certainly make it harder for South Korean workers to secure and defend their rights to livable jobs and wages.

China's new economic strategy poses a danger to the South Korean economy in yet another way. The South Korean economy has long been highly dependent on exports, and has become even more so since the 1997–98 crisis. To this point, South Korea has succeeded in running a trade surplus with China. Some argue that this trade surplus will grow even larger as South Korean investment in China encourages new exports through intra-firm trade channels. In reality, however, any such gains are likely to soon be outweighed by export losses resulting from China's production and export of goods that South Korea currently exports to China and third countries.

While China and South Korea initially enjoyed a complementary trading relationship, the two countries are now trading almost equally in a number of areas, including steel and petrochemicals. A case in point:

> Exports of heavy industry goods to Korea accounted for 1 percent of China's overall exports in 1992, but now account for 47 percent. China is Korea's second largest source of steel imports, but also its number one market for steel and petrochemicals. Korea retains an advantage in information technology—16 percent of all Korean exports to China—but appears to be losing ground in textiles. According to KITA [the Korean International Trade Association], China is Korea's largest source of textile imports.[50]

According to the Korea Economic Institute, a South Korean government supported, U.S.-based research institute, "Within the next decade, Chinese firms are expected to out-compete Korean producers of low-end electronics equipment at home and abroad. Institutes and business organizations already report drops in domestic sales of Korean home appliance products."[51] Studies by private and state research institutes in Korea raise the same warning, that "China's export competitiveness was in some cases greater than that of Korea in sectors such as machinery, electronics/home appliances, textiles, and some information products. Studies also considered the implications for Korea of China's WTO entry, and predicted that China would attract FDI away from Korea and increase its competitiveness and global market share in agriculture and home appliances."[52]

China's efforts to protect its foreign-based producers represent another threat to South Korean exports. For example:

> China in recent years has resorted to applying antidumping duties to Korean imports to stem dumping and an increase in competition from Korean firms.

During 2002, its first year in the WTO, China initiated a significant number of dumping investigations of Korean products. China has restricted or has threatened to restrict a number of Korea's top exports—polyester staple fiber, textiles (coated art paper), and steel. The MOCIE [Ministry of Commerce, Industry and Energy] report on Korea's export competitiveness in China reveals a correlation between an increase in the number of such dumping investigations of Korean imports to a rise in China of the competitiveness of foreign manufacturers of the same products.[53]

In sum, China's economic transformation poses a serious challenge to South Korea's economy. China is increasingly attracting South Korean investment and producing products that are likely to compete favorably with South Korean exports in home and third-country markets. Mainstream economists argue that South Korea can avoid the resulting premature hollowing out of its economy by relying on market forces to encourage technological upgrading to higher value added exports. This, of course, means that South Korea must attract substantial new foreign investment, something that the country has failed to achieve despite government attempts to weaken the trade union movement.

The most likely outcome of current regional and international dynamics is that the South Korean economy will become more narrowly export focused and tied to China's economic future. This will leave it more unbalanced and unstable, and far less able to support any broad-based improvement in living and working conditions for the great majority of South Korean workers.

JAPAN

According to the World Bank, Japan should be one of Asia's biggest beneficiaries from China's growing export success and membership in the WTO.[54] Chinese-Japanese trade is growing rapidly, topping $100 billion for the first time in 2002. Japanese exports to China soared 28.2 percent to $39.9 billion in 2002. China is now the second biggest market for Japanese exports, behind the United States. China is also the world's largest exporter to Japan, having overtaken the United States in 2002, when its exports to Japan reached $61.7

billion.[55] Predictions are that trade between the two countries will continue to rise at a rapid pace for the next few years.

China's growth is currently creating opportunities for the Japanese economy for two main reasons. First, "for the moment," the Chinese and Japanese economies "are roughly complementary. China specializes in labor-intensive products and Japan excels in high-technology goods that require capital and design expertise."[56] As a result, "the areas of head-to-head industrial competition are still relatively few—around 16 percent. In 2002, China accounted for only 17.8 percent of Japan's total imports, or approximately 1.3 percent of Japan's GDP."[57]

Second, "Japan is a big capital goods exporter, and there is a capital spending boom going on in China."[58] "Orders from China are a big part of the resurgence in demand for the materials, capital equipment and [high-end] consumer electronics that Japan still produces better than anyone else does."[59] These orders have assisted the (still hesitant) recovery of the Japanese economy from the 2001 recession.

Unfortunately, ongoing trade and investment dynamics are working to ensure that it is only the dominant Japanese firms, and not the majority of Japanese working people, that will actually benefit from the developing division of labor between China and Japan. The range of products (and employment opportunities) in which Japan has a competitive advantage over China is rapidly narrowing. "China is no longer just about vast pools of cheap labor, it is increasingly about the combination of that with skilled human capital."[60] Even more important, a growing percentage of the products exported from China to Japan are produced with Japanese components and/or by Japanese firms operating in China. Japanese capital has, in fact, established a major industrial presence in China, and this presence is growing rapidly. Already, by 2000, Japan had 772 production facilities in China, compared with only 692 in the United States.[61] "As of 2001, Japan [had] invested $32.3 billion in China, not counting Hong Kong and Macao, making it the second-largest investor in mainland China after the United States."[62]

Although this foreign investment dynamic is currently helping boost Japan's exports of capital goods and components to China, this boost is largely a temporary "set-up effect" that will, from the standpoint of the Japanese economy as opposed to Japanese capital, eventually be more than offset by the loss of export markets and intensified import competition. The Japanese economy experienced two similar short-term recoveries from its stagnation, first after the high-yen crisis of 1985 and again in the years just prior to the 1997–98 East Asian crisis, both buoyed by exports of capital goods and components to offshore export platforms in Southeast Asia (as well as to the United States, where Japanese auto firms in particular were setting up new production facilities).[63] Like these earlier two episodes, the construction of a new export platform in China is likely to leave the Japanese economy with a narrower range of internationally competitive goods-producing sectors capable of generating decent job opportunities.

Indeed, the shift of Japanese production to China and neighboring countries was an important determinant of the drop in Japanese manufacturing employment from 15.7 million in 1992 to 14.6 million in 1995, and to 13 million in 2001.[64] Both this trend of job loss and China's central role in it are expected to continue, as the *New York Times* explains:

> [In spring 2001], Toshiba Corp. stopped making television sets in Japan, turning to its factories in China to supply the home market. Soon after, Minolta Co. announced that it was phasing out camera production in Japan and would import from Shanghai instead....Just last month, like falling dominoes, several other Japanese manufacturers announced plans to import bicycles, motorcycles, buses and cell phones from their Chinese factories...."We look at China as the most important growth market," said Yukio Shotoku, overseas managing director for Matsushita Electric Works Ltd. His company is closing 11 factories and pushing 8,000 workers into early retirement in Japan, whose labor costs he described as "the biggest headache...." In the last decade, Japanese investment in China has doubled, to the point where more than half of China-Japan trade is conducted among Japanese companies.[65]

And as China's economic restructuring continues, additional sectors of the Japanese economy are likely to be regionalized. For example, Japan's automobile industry is expected to undergo a major transformation, as Japanese producers reorganize their production system to incorporate China. "Under WTO rules, China's tariffs on automobiles will be slashed 25 percent by 2006 and import restrictions will be ended. For this reason, the Japanese auto industry is also now moving aggressively into China, where, in addition to access for that longer-term domestic Chinese auto market, it can save 10 to 20 percent on manufacturing costs for its exports."[66] The World Bank predicts that one result of this move will be a major contraction of automobile production in Japan.[67]

Japanese workers obviously cannot compete against Chinese production, when "a Chinese factory worker, just a short freighter trip away...will work two days for the same pay that some Japanese workers earn in one hour."[68] And the further regionalization of Japanese production can be expected to leave the economy even more export oriented and unbalanced and intensify existing Japanese employment and wage problems.[69]

As with earlier restructuring episodes in the 1970s, '80s, and '90s, the movement of Japanese industrial capital to China will not even reduce Japan's dependence on extra-regional markets—especially the United States. Rather, with China's exports (like those of the four "little tigers" and the ASEAN-3 before it) increasingly reliant on the U.S. market, Japan's export-base, insofar as it is oriented toward China, will still rely on U.S. demand for imports. Japan's growth will thus remain susceptible to fluctuations of the U.S. economy as well as to long-run problems (including protectionist pressures) stemming from the unsustainability of the massive U.S. trade deficit.

NORTH AMERICA

We have focused on regional developments because analysts favorable to the Chinese model argue that China can serve as the new locomotive to reenergize East Asian growth. In debunking this notion we could have easily extended our analysis to show how China's emergence as an export-platform for transnational capital generates new tensions for workers elsewhere, including in North America.

For example, China has been greatly increasing its market share in the United States at the expense of Mexico. According to *Business Week*:

Right now, Mexico is the No. 2 exporter to the U.S. after Canada. But barring a huge SARS-related setback, China will wrest away that title sometime this year

[2003]....That is a devastating reversal of fortune for a country that for the past decade has enjoyed privileged access to the world's biggest market under the North American Free Trade Agreement. "We're in trouble. China is growing so fast. They have cheap labor, and they give companies a lot of incentives to invest there," says Oscar Garcia, manager of the Melco Display Devices plant in Mexicali. The factory, which is owned by Japan's Mitsubishi Corp. and churns out cathode-ray tubes used in computer monitors, will close at the end of July. That's because it can no longer complete with lower-priced Chinese production.[70]

Employment in the *maquiladora* industry in 2003 was down nearly 20 percent from its 2000 peak of 1.4 million.[71] This drop was only partly due to the U.S. recession: while Mexican exports to the United States showed virtually zero growth in 2002, China's grew by 20 percent.[72] An equally, if not more important explanation, is that growing numbers of *maquiladora* producers are shifting their production to China. Among other things, they are in search of even cheaper wages: "An assembly-line worker in Guadalajara earns $2.50 to $3.50 an hour; his counterpart in Guangdong makes 50 cents to 80 cents."[73]

"Mexico has nearly lost the battle on low-skilled, labor-intensive industries, where it simply cannot compete with China on labor costs and will likely continue losing market share," says Merrill Lynch.[74] The Mexican government now seeks to stop the bleeding by creating even more profitable conditions for foreign production, and largely at the expense of workers.[75] In sum, Mexico's own foreign-dominated, export-led growth strategy is now in crisis, in large part because developments in China created conditions that were even more attractive to foreign capital.

Workers in the United States also are struggling to defend themselves against competitive pressures generated by the Chinese growth strategy. The U.S. trade deficit with China reached $103 billion in 2002, with U.S. exports equal to just $22 billion and Chinese exports equal to $125 billion. "The numbers are eye-opening. Chinese exports soared 22 percent [in 2002]. And it is not just low-cost towels. Exports of computer and telecom products are growing 60 percent annually."[76]

The growth of manufacturing FDI in China has, as we have seen, transformed the nature of Chinese exports. China's exports to the

United States are increasingly of a kind that threatens even higher-waged workers.[77] "Although in 1989 only 30% of imports from China competed against goods produced by high-wage industries in the U.S. market, by 1999 that percentage had risen to 50%."[78] One result is that "manufacturing businesses from electronics to furniture and fishing lures are closing their doors or moving production to China."[79]

A major reason that China now runs the largest trade surplus of any country with the United States is that many Asian producers who used to export to the United States from other countries in Asia are now producing and exporting from China. Of course, U.S. corporations are also taking advantage of opportunities in China, greatly increasing their investments there. As the *Financial Times* observes: "While many small enterprises and textile manufacturers are suffering from competition with China, large U.S. companies such as GM, GE, DuPont, and Yum Brands, which includes KFC, are thriving on the mainland."[80] In many cases, this investment directly adds to the growing U.S. trade deficit with China. "Over the course of a few years, U.S. multinationals operating in China have turned from net exporters to China to net exporters to the United States, a gap that will only widen with increased FDI to China, further contributing to the growing United States trade deficit."[81] This helps explain why the U.S. trade deficit with China has continued to grow despite the more rapid growth of the Chinese economy compared to the United States.[82]

Although profitable for some of the largest American companies, the economic transformation of China and its export successes are far from positive for working people and economic security and stability in the United States. They have contributed to the destruction of U.S. manufacturing production and jobs, the decline in U.S. living and working conditions, and greater economic imbalance and instability in the United States and world economy.

THE BANKRUPTCY OF MAINSTREAM REFORM PROPOSALS

Capitalism's inability to provide alternatives to the competitive race to the bottom generated by export-led growth is highlighted by the strategic proposals made by the few mainstream economists who recognize the international contradictions created by China's export success. Consider the explanation of Pierre Goad, a *Far Eastern Economic Review* columnist, as to "why China doesn't really have any choice but to adopt a consumer-led model":

> It's simply too big to copy the export-led model of its neighbors. South Korea's 47 million people exported $31.2 billion worth of goods to the U.S. last year [1999]. If Chinese exports per worker reached Korean levels, China would have exported $837 billion of goods to the U.S. last year—or 83% of worldwide exports to the U.S. That's not going to happen.[83]

Goad's observation is a sound one, but his projection of a new "consumer-led" growth path is contradicted by China's growing dependence on exports. And Goad does not explain how mass consumption can possibly take up the slack created by a reversal of these export trends, given the accelerating inequality of income distribution generated by China's capitalist transformation which erodes the basis for a mass working-class market.

Indeed, with the purchasing power of the majority of rural people stagnating, with intensified exploitation and repression of industrial workers, and with the plunder of state assets by the new capitalist class and its Chinese Communist Party allies, the country's household income inequality now exceeds that of India and Indonesia and rivals that of Brazil and South Africa.[84] As the *New York Times* reports, "Some corporate leaders remain skeptical that spending on cell phones and other consumer items can move much higher in an economy where industrial workers still count themselves lucky if they earn more than $200 a month. 'As long as the wages are so low, it will be difficult to increase consumption,' says Hans-Jorg Bullinger, the president of Fraunhofer-Gesellschaft, a big German contract research company."[85]

A more basic problem with capitalist consumption-led growth proposals is their presumption that problems of overproduction and export-dependency reflect simple policy errors or misguided forecasts on the part of firms, rather than the fundamental laws of motion of competitive capital accumulation. Mainstream analysts do not even pause to reflect on the *coexistence* of overproduction (as reflected in deflation and burgeoning excess capacity, especially in consumer durables industries) and the rising export-intensity of China's growth as a possible symptom of some deeper malfunction, especially given the *coterminous* rise of inequality. In reality, as China's experience so powerfully demonstrates, overproduction and export-dependency are twin outcomes of capitalism's tendency to develop productive forces only in and through the exploitation of labor and its natural and social conditions, a process that constrains the growth of the mass market relative to productive capacity.

From this perspective, the likely outcome of any "consumer-led" strategy within China's capitalist transformation will not be a balanced and sustainable growth path, but rather the *overlaying* of consumer goods production for the capitalist and petit bourgeois elite onto the continued reliance on FDI and exports as the fundamental engines of growth—a pattern that will continue to place downward pressures on the majority's work and living conditions in both China and the nations that compete with it. The Chinese government may keep trying to ameliorate the overproduction tendency by boosting its spending and taking a lax attitude toward credit expansion (while continuing on with the capitalist reforms that underpin overproduction itself). But the limits of such pump-priming in the absence of a viable mass working-class market were already evident by the fall of 2003, in the form of the continued buildup of excess capacity, as well as the absorption of positive demand impulses by a nationwide speculative boom in the real estate sector—with massive overbuilding of luxury and semi-luxury housing as well as commercial structures.[86]

CONCLUSION

In highlighting the destructive impact of China's economic transformation, we do not mean to argue that Chinese workers are now the main cause of economic and social problems for working people in East Asia and beyond. As we have seen, China's rapid export growth has come at high expense for Chinese working people themselves, and it has even failed to sustain any growth in manufacturing job opportunities for Chinese workers. That China has not been "stealing jobs" from other countries' workers is clear from official Chinese government data indicating that the country's total manufacturing employment, after rising from 83.5 million in 1985 to 109.6 million in 1995, declined to only 83.1 million in 2002.[87]

The fact is that in China and throughout the capitalist world, the competitive drive for profit has an inbuilt tendency to eliminate jobs through the mechanization and intensification of labor, and through overproduction and resulting recessions and economic retrenchment. In China this tendency is taking the form of restructurings, privatizations, and closures of state enterprises. In the United States, meanwhile, much of the recent shrinkage of manufacturing employment has been due to the 2000–2001 recession "and rapidly rising American productivity that makes it possible to churn out more goods with fewer people," although industrial capital flight and import pressures have also been important factors.[88] As Karl Marx once observed, "The industrial war of capitalists among themselves...has the peculiarity that the battles in it are won less by recruiting than by discharging the army of workers. The generals (the capitalists) vie with one another as to who can discharge the greatest number of industrial workers."[89]

In short, far from bashing China, our aim here is to demonstrate that China's *capitalist growth strategy* generates regional and global as well as national contradictions. Insofar as it ties the entire East Asian region more tightly to an export-led growth strategy, China's transformation worsens the dangers of overproduction and instability. Export-led growth pushes down regional wage rates, undermines domestic consumption, and generates destructive regional competition for foreign investment and export production. It also depends more and more on the ability of the United States to consume greater and greater amounts of imports. New crises grow increasingly likely under these conditions. The danger, of course, is that workers in different countries will come to see each other as the enemy rather than the system of capitalism that shapes their relationships and pits them against each other in a destructive competition.

5

China and Socialism: Conclusion

We have argued that it is wrong to celebrate China as an economic success story or development model. But why is it so important how socialists and other progressives understand China? Is this all just an academic desire to properly interpret the Chinese experience, or a political sectarianism based on an *a priori* notion of "pure" socialism? The answer is no; the stakes are arguably much higher and more meaningful.

First, as we have seen, treating China as a success story tends to draw attention away from the uneven and combined development of capitalism. The search for national models based on national economic and competitive criteria implicitly suggests that different countries can simultaneously achieve China-like economic successes based on their simultaneous adoption of China-like economic policies. But this is a fallacy of composition insofar as China's growth has been based on historically specific conditions that have allowed it to attract abundant foreign investment and maintain very low wages—conditions that include the contradictory development of capitalism in other countries.

China's growth has been both cause and effect of the growing problems of FDI- and export-led growth in East Asia and Mexico, as well as of the contradictions of capitalist "maturation" in the developed countries, especially Japan and the United States. Its national

competitiveness should not blind us to the fact that its rapid industrialization has been part and parcel of the uneven development and
overproduction of capital on a world scale. Unfortunately, when progressives engage in a shared competitive search with neoliberals for
national economic successes (and failures), they end up evaluating
individual countries in isolation from the wider logic and dynamics
of capitalism, or uncritically taking the latter as natural givens. The
case of China shows how this approach can lead to progressive support for policies and regimes that are destructive of the interests of
working people.

Second, the Chinese experience demonstrates that market
reforms have a dynamic of their own. China's overall transition from
decentralization to FDI- and export-led growth was driven by an
internal set of pressures. In other words, while some have argued that
China illustrates the viability and attractiveness of market socialism, in
reality the Chinese experience reveals that market socialism is an
unstable formation whose internal logic tends to marginalize socialism in favor of the market and the full restoration of capitalism.

This brings us to our third point, which is that the identification of
China as a success story leads to an acceptance of export-led development as a "sound" and even "progressive" development strategy. But
to celebrate China's highly competitive export orientation, and the
FDI and domestic marketization that brought it about, is to legitimize
neoliberal criteria of success. This tendency to define progressive in
terms of mainstream notions of success parallels the opportunistic
manipulation of Marxism by Chinese government leaders, as shown
by their sequential reinvention of the core of socialism in Chinese
practice—from the iron rice bowl and the communes to the central
role of state enterprises, to the continued importance of the "public
sector" (including quasi-collective enterprises), and finally to the leading role of the Communist Party itself (specifically of party officers)
regardless of the reality of capitalist economic relations.

Such ideological manipulation purges concrete class analysis
from Marxism, converting it into a font of transhistorical "wisdom"
at the service of elites.[1] Marx himself warned Russian socialists
about those who would distort his approach into a "master key," i.e.,

"a general historico-philosophical theory, the supreme virtue of which consists in being supra-historical."[2]

Fourth, by measuring "progress" in terms of mainstream criteria of success, leftists tend to discount the importance of the various social ramifications of Chinese policy. The growing unemployment, inequality, and insecurity; the cutbacks of communal health care and education; the worsening oppression of women; the marginalization of agriculture; and the multiplication of environmental crises; all of these come to be treated as inessential side effects rather than essential preconditions and inevitable outcomes of China's capitalist development.

In attempting to out-neoliberal the neoliberals, progressives lose sight of the basic Marxist observation that capitalist development involves the social separation of workers from the necessary conditions of production, including natural conditions, and the conversion of these conditions and of workers' labor power into means of producing commodities for a profit. In other words, they lose sight of the fact that capitalist production is class-alienated, class-exploitative production. One consequence is that they forget to consider the critical question of whether contemporary capitalist production, given its highly socialized, biospheric, and resource-intensive character, is capable of achieving success in terms of the sustainable development of productive forces (human, social, and ecological) on a global scale. This causes them to overlook the fact that the creative element of capitalism's "creative destruction" is now far outweighed by the destructive element, especially once one takes the global socio-economic and ecological "side effects" of national capitalist successes into account. Thus, the poster-country game in development studies is not neutral, but instead strongly favors neoliberalism, especially as it submerges such concerns.

Fifth, the slide into acceptance of capitalist development criteria undermines international solidarity. Let us suppose that Chinese workers and communities begin to more effectively challenge not only their political repression but also the marketization and capitalization of their conditions, as we should hope they do. If this challenge is waged against a system that non-Chinese leftists have endorsed as socialist or progressive, these leftists will be in no position to offer these Chinese workers support.

Indeed, the combination of the Chinese government's elite-man-agement interpretation of socialism and foreign leftist endorsements of China's "socialist market economy" could easily lead Chinese worker-activists to reject socialism altogether. At a minimum, this sit-uation can be expected to create tensions and confusions between these activists and an international left-intellectual community likely to resent their resistance (or find it difficult to acknowledge) because it undermines its chosen model. Such is the political cost of formulat-ing progressive development models based on elite-driven strategies for successful insertion into the global-capitalist system.

As David McNally emphasizes, "Revolutionary politics begins... with the common sense of the working class" and must "try to draw out and systematize the worldview which is implicit in [working-class] practices of resistance," especially those "popular genres which entail solidarity, cooperation, and egalitarianism."[3] Instead of building models of progressive capitalism out of the experiences of the latest poster countries, left activist-intellectuals should act as "the force that generalizes experiences of opposition into an increas-ingly systematic program, the force that challenges the traditional and dominant ideas inherited by workers (patriotism, sexism, racism, etc.) by showing how they conflict with the interests and aspirations implicit in resistance to exploitation and oppression."[4]

Rooting our development visions and policy programs in the strug-gles of worker-community movements will not eliminate all disagree-ments (far from it!), but it is more likely to be a popularly resonant strategy characterized by solidarity than the search for progressive national-capitalist successes. To endorse China's growth successes, in particular, is to endorse a development model that pits Chinese work-ers against workers in other countries in a competitive race to the bot-tom that has nothing to do with any progressive development of pro-ductive forces holistically considered. This cannot be the basis for building socialism or forwarding socialist values of sustainability, equality, solidarity, and democracy.

To better illustrate the nature of the choices we face, we conclude this book by highlighting some basic principles of this alternative approach to building development visions. We start with the recognition that both the East Asian crisis and China's capitalist restoration have promoted widespread struggles by working people to resist capitalist and government efforts to have them shoulder the main burden of the crisis and restructuring costs. Although these struggles have so far been largely defensive and fragmented in nature, they have prevented the full implementation of IMF-style liberalization and austerity policies in the ASEAN countries and South Korea, toppled the brutal Suharto dictatorship in Indonesia, and forced China's government to pay at least some attention to the country's developing health and social welfare crisis. Implicit in all these struggles is a general resistance to the determination of work and living conditions by market and profit criteria, rather than by human needs.

If there is any hope for a more progressive form of development and integration in the China–East Asia region, it lies in these militant tendencies created by the region's industrialization. Taken individually, it is true that national working-class movements are in a relatively weak position to push through a popular structural transformation. But if they are able to coalesce, their ability to envision and fight for human need–based forms of regional development will be greatly strengthened. Significantly, we see the potential for such a regionalization of class struggle growing as a result of China's emergence, precisely because that emergence deepens the capitalist regionalization process, thereby increasingly subjecting workers throughout the region to a common set of competitive pressures that could enable them to find common ground for their nationally based struggles.

In this view, the problem faced by workers is not export production per se, but rather the absence of alternatives to profit-driven export activity—alternatives that serve the needs of human development. In other words, trade itself is not the problem. A strategy firmly anchored in basic human needs, and gradually expanding into other, secondary needs of human development, would no doubt require imports and lead to the creation of exportable goods and services. Thus, it is possible to imagine an alternative mode of exporting and regional economic interaction emerging out of an autocentric integration of domestic needs, domestic demand, and domestic resource use.[5] By contrast, capitalist export-led development policies, such as those that drove the East Asian "miracles" and China's economic transformation, lead to national integration into transnational dominated production networks, intensified competition among workers, and the reshaping of domestic social institutions (education, health care, legal systems, environmental regulations, etc.) in line with the market's monetary criteria and competitiveness imperatives.

For example, the creation of a national health-care system would require developing a construction industry to build clinics and hospitals, a drug industry to treat illnesses, a machine-tool industry to make equipment, a software industry for record keeping, an educational system to train doctors and nurses, etc., all shaped by the developing needs and capabilities of the people on local, national, and regional levels. The requisite mobilization of resources and technical and institutional innovations would clearly hinge upon a high degree of popular enthusiasm for and participation in the development process.

Should these conditions be met, it is conceivable that certain parts of such a popularly based health complex might develop a significant export capability. The cultivation of health-system capacities would also likely require some imports and investment agreements with foreign enterprises in order to overcome particular resource and/or technological bottlenecks. This trade and foreign investment would assist the development of locally planned products and processes responsive to grassroots health-care needs and capabilities, rather than simply harnessing the economy to products and processes developed by transnational capital. Cuba's health-care, biotechnology, and pharmaceutical sectors, developed in the face of the U.S. embargo, illustrate the practical possibilities and problems in this area.[6]

Health care is just one example of how a development strategy rooted in working peoples' needs and capabilities need not be an autarkic fantasy. International trade need not reduce people and communities to mere conditions of commodity production for profit insofar as exports and imports are an outgrowth of a resource allocation and investment process commanded by popular and human developmental needs. What is important is that production be driven by use values that are socially agreed upon, not by the requirements of class-exploitative monetary accumulation.

Of course, the human and natural resource base of the country involved will also shape the exact pattern of development. This makes it all the more important for this needs-based strategy to be implemented in a plurality of countries that can develop trade and investment relations among themselves as an outgrowth of developing productive capabilities rooted in their own specific historical, cultural, and resource "endowments" (and class struggles).

Such a shared and complementary development process would be a far cry from the activities and relationships promoted by neoliberal export-led development strategies. The neoliberal approach precludes popular mobilization and participation in investment and resource allocation, and promotes a destructive competition among workers and nations—one that accentuates capital's built-in tendencies toward unequal development, overproduction, and crises.[7]

In sum, that it is necessary to engage progressives in debate over the nature of the Chinese economic experience and argue for a new approach to development based on the above principles shows that we have much work to do to reclaim the power of Marxism to expose the contradictory workings and exploitative nature of global capitalism. As we have seen, the continuing celebration of the Chinese economic model has real political consequences. These consequences make it painfully clear that this effort is not a mere abstract-theoretical endeavor, but rather a critical concrete task for those of us seeking to build a new and better world.

APPENDIX

TABLE 1: Real GDP and Export Indicators for China

YEAR	Annual Growth of Real GDP(%)	Annual Growth of Exports (%)*	Ratio of Exports/GDP (%)
1985	13.5	4.6	9.0
1986	8.9	11.5	10.5
1987	11.6	27.5	12.3
1988	11.3	20.5	11.8
1989	4.1	10.6	11.7
1990	3.8	18.2	16.0
1991	9.2	15.7	17.7
1992	14.2	18.2	17.6
1993	13.5	8.0	15.3
1994	12.6	31.9	22.3
1995	10.5	23.0	21.2
1996	9.6	1.5	18.5
1997	8.8	21.0	20.4
1998	7.8	0.5	19.4
1999	7.1	6.1	19.7
2000	8.0	27.8	23.1
2001	7.3	6.8	23.0
2002	8.0	22.1	26.2

* $US, FOB.

SOURCE: National Bureau of Statistics of China, *China Statistical Yearbook 2002* (Beijing: China Statistics Press, 2002); Asian Development Bank, *Key Indicators 2002*, http://www.adb.org, and *Asian Recovery Information Center Indicators*, 2003, http://aric.adb.org.

TABLE 2: FDI Indicators for China

YEAR	FDI ($US billion)	Annual FDI Growth (%)	Ratio (%) of FDI to Gross Investment
1985	1.03	-8.4	1.1
1986	1.43	38.3	1.6
1987	1.67	17.1	1.7
1988	2.34	40.4	1.9
1989	2.61	11.5	2.3
1990	3.49	33.7	3.5
1991	4.37	25.2	3.9
1992	11.01	151.9	7.3
1993	27.52	150.0	12.3
1994	33.77	22.7	17.3
1995	37.52	11.1	15.4
1996	41.73	11.2	14.9
1997	45.28	8.5	14.9
1998	45.46	0.4	13.6
1999	40.29	-11.4	11.3
2000	40.80	1.3	10.4
2001	46.77	14.6	10.5
2002	52.77	12.8	10.4

NOTE: FDI is measured on a net balance of payments basis. Gross investment is gross fixed capital formation, including residential and nonresidential structures.

SOURCE: National Bureau of Statistics of China, *China Statistical Yearbook 2002* (Beijing: China Statistics Press, 2002); Asian Development Bank, *Key Indicators 2002*, and *Key Indicators 2003*, www.adb.org.

TABLE 3: State and Urban Collective Enterprise Shares in Total Employment

YEAR	State Enterprise Shares (%)			Urban Collective Shares (%)		
	Manu-facturing	Domestic Trade	Urban Residents	Manu-facturing	Domestic Trade	Urban Residents
1978	45.9	79.6	78.3	21.5	15.1	21.5
1980	44.1	73.7	76.2	22.8	17.2	23.0
1985	40.1	34.7	70.2	21.7	31.1	26.0
1990	39.4	33.4	60.7	20.6	26.8	20.8
1991	39.4	33.1	61.1	20.2	26.2	20.8
1992	38.7	32.3	61.0	19.2	24.8	20.3
1993	37.1	29.3	59.8	17.2	21.5	18.6
1994	34.6	26.9	60.1	15.8	18.3	17.6
1995	34.0	24.7	59.1	14.5	16.2	16.5
1996	33.0	23.4	56.4	13.8	14.8	15.1
1997	31.3	21.6	53.1	12.9	13.3	13.9
1998	22.6	14.9	41.9	8.9	8.9	9.1
1999	20.3	12.8	38.2	7.7	7.3	7.6
2000	17.6	11.3	35.0	6.5	6.1	6.5
2001	14.8	9.4	31.9	5.3	4.6	5.4

NOTE: Domestic trade includes wholesale and retail trade plus eating and drinking places.

SOURCE: National Bureau of Statistics of China, *China Statistical Yearbook 2002* (Beijing: China Statistics Press, 2002).

TABLE 4: Township and Village Enterprise (TVE) Employment

YEAR	Number Employed in TVEs (millions)	TVE Share of Rural Employment (%)	TVE Share of National Employment (%)
1978	28.3	9.2	7.0
1980	30.0	9.4	7.1
1985	69.8	18.8	14.0
1987	88.1	22.6	16.7
1988	95.5	23.8	17.6
1989	93.7	22.9	16.9
1990	92.7	19.6	14.5
1991	96.1	20.1	14.8
1992	106.3	22.0	16.2
1993	123.5	25.3	18.6
1994	120.2	24.6	17.9
1995	128.6	26.3	18.9
1996	135.1	27.6	19.6
1997	130.5	26.6	18.8
1998	125.4	25.6	17.9
1999	127.0	25.9	18.0
2000	128.2	26.2	17.8
2001	130.9	26.7	17.9

SOURCE: Ming Lu, Jianyong Fan, Shejian Liu and Yan Yan, "Employment Restructuring During China's Economic Transition," *Monthly Labor Review* 125, no. 8.(August 2002); National Bureau of Statistics of China, *China Statistical Yearbook 2002* (Beijing: China Statistics Press, 2002).

TABLE 5: Share of Foreign Affiliates in Total Manufacturing Sales of China

YEAR	1990	1991	1992	1993	1994	1995	1996	1997	1998	1999	2000
Share (%)	2.3	5.3	7.1	9.1	11.3	14.3	15.1	18.6	24.3	27.7	31.3

SOURCE: UNCTAD, *World Investment Report 2002: Transnational Corporations and Export Competitiveness* (New York: United Nations, 2002).

TABLE 6: Foreign-Funded Enterprise Shares in Exports
and Total Trade of China

YEAR	Share of Exports (%)	Share of Total Trade (%)
1990	17.4	12.6
1991	21.4	16.8
1992	26.3	20.5
1993	34.3	27.5
1994	37.0	28.7
1995	39.1	31.5
1996	47.3	40.7
1997	47.0	41.0
1998	46.7	44.1
1999	48.4	45.5
2000	49.9	47.9
2001	50.8	50.1

SOURCE: Chen Zhilong, "Two Decades of Utilizing FDI in China: States, Structure and Impact," *China Report* 38, no. 4 (2002); National Bureau of Statistics of China, *China Statistical Yearbook 2002* (Beijing: China Statistics Press, 2002).

TABLE 7: Inflation and Unemployment in China

YEAR	Annual Inflation of Consumer Prices (%)	Unemployment Rate In Urban Areas (%)	YEAR	Annual Inflation of Consumer Prices (%)	Unemployment Rate In Urban Areas (%)
1985	9.3	1.8	1994	24.1	2.8
1986	6.5	2.0	1995	17.1	2.9
1987	7.3	2.0	1996	8.3	3.0
1988	18.8	2.0	1997	2.8	3.1
1989	18.0	2.6	1998	-0.8	3.1
1990	3.1	2.5	1999	-1.4	3.1
1991	3.4	2.3	2000	0.3	3.1
1992	6.4	2.3	2001	0.9	3.6
1993	14.7	2.6	2002	-0.8	4.0

SOURCE: National Bureau of Statistics of China, *China Statistical Yearbook 2002* (Beijing: China Statistics Press, 2002); Asian Development Bank, *Key Indicators 2002* (www.adb.org) and *Asian Recovery Information Center Indicators*, 2003 (http://aric.adb.org).

TABLE 8: Unemployment Rate in Urban Areas:
Official Versus Estimated Actual Rates

YEAR	Official Rate (%)	Estimated Actual Rate (%)	YEAR	Official Rate (%)	Estimated Actual Rate (%)
1993	2.6	3.3–3.7	1996	3.0	5.1–6.0
1994	2.8	3.6–4.1	1997	3.1	6.8–7.8
1995	2.9	4.4–5.0	1998	3.1	7.9–8.3

SOURCE: Social and Economic Policy Institute, "Overview of Current Labor Market Conditions in China," January 2002, http://www.sepi.org.

TABLE 9: Aggregate and Sectoral Employment (millions)
and Sectoral Shares in Aggregate Employment

YEAR	Aggregate Employ-ment	Agriculture		Manufacturing*		Other**	
		Employed	Share	Employed	Share	Employed	Share
1985	498.73	311.30	62.4%	83.49	16.7%	103.94	20.8%
1986	512.82	312.54	60.9%	89.80	17.5%	110.48	21.5%
1987	527.83	316.63	60.0%	93.43	17.7%	117.77	22.3%
1988	543.34	322.49	59.4%	96.61	17.8%	124.24	22.9%
1989	553.29	332.25	60.0%	95.68	17.3%	125.36	22.7%
1990	639.09	341.17	53.4%	96.98	15.2%	200.94	31.4%
1991	647.99	349.56	53.9%	99.47	15.4%	198.96	30.7%
1992	655.54	347.95	53.1%	102.19	15.6%	205.40	31.3%
1993	663.73	339.66	51.2%	104.67	15.8%	219.40	33.1%
1994	671.99	333.86	49.7%	107.74	16.0%	230.39	34.3%
1995	679.47	330.18	48.6%	109.63	16.1%	239.36	35.2%
1996	688.50	329.10	47.8%	109.38	15.9%	250.02	36.3%
1997	698.20	330.95	47.4%	107.63	15.4%	259.62	37.2%
1998	706.37	332.32	47.0%	93.23	13.2%	280.82	39.8%
1999	713.94	334.93	46.9%	90.61	12.7%	288.40	40.4%
2000	720.85	333.55	46.3%	89.24	12.4%	298.06	41.3%
2001	730.25	329.74	45.2%	89.32	12.2%	311.19	42.6%
2002	737.40	324.57	44.1%	83.08	11.3%	329.45	44.7%

* Includes mining and utilities. ** Includes construction.

SOURCE: Asian Development Bank, *Key Indicators 2002*, www.adb.org; Asian Development Bank, *Key Indicators 2003*, www.adb.org.

TABLE 10: Net FDI in China and Other East Asian Countries ($US billion)

Country	1997	1998	1999	2000	2001	2002
China (PRC)	45.28	45.46	40.29	40.80	46.77	52.77
Hong Kong	–.–	-2.22	5.21	2.57	12.43	-3.98
Taiwan	-3.00	-3.61	-1.49	-1.77	-1.37	-3.44
Singapore	4.45	7.14	7.83	6.40	1.32	1.97
South Korea	-1.61	0.67	5.14	4.28	1.11	-0.70
Indonesia	4.68	-0.36	-2.75	-4.55	-5.88	-7.07
Thailand	3.30	7.36	5.74	3.37	3.65	0.86
Malaysia	5.56	2.19	2.32	1.76	0.29	1.30
Philippines	1.11	1.59	1.92	1.45	1.14	1.03

SOURCE: Asian Development Bank, *Key Indicators 2002*, *Key Indicators 2003* (www.adb.org) and *Asian Recovery Information Center Indicators* (http://aric.adb.org). The PRC data are an updated version of those provided in the National Bureau of Statistics of China, *China Statistical Yearbook 2002* (Beijing: China Statistics Press, 2002).

TABLE 11: Total Exports ($US billion, with % shares
of each exporting country in grand total)

Country	1985	1990	1995	1998	1999	2000	2001	2002
China	27.33	62.76	148.96	183.74	194.93	249.20	266.14	371.42
(PRC)	(14.6)	(15.0)	(17.0)	(20.0)	(20.0)	(21.2)	(24.2)	(31.3)
Hong Kong	30.18	82.14	173.56	173.69	173.79	201.99	189.84	139.50
	(16.1)	(19.6)	(20.0)	(18.9)	(17.8)	(17.2)	(17.2)	(11.8)
Taiwan	30.73	67.21	111.66	110.58	121.59	148.32	122.87	130.60
	(16.4)	(16.0)	(12.7)	(12.1)	(12.5)	(12.6)	(11.2)	(11.0)
Singapore	22.81	52.75	118.19	109.89	114.73	137.93	121.72	125.09
	(11.9)	(12.6)	(13.5)	(12.0)	(11.8)	(11.7)	(11.1)	(10.5)
South Korea	30.29	67.81	131.31	132.70	143.65	171.83	149.84	153.28
	(16.2)	(16.2)	(15.0)	(14.5)	(14.7)	(14.6)	(13.6)	(12.9)
Indonesia	18.60	25.68	45.43	48.84	48.65	62.10	64.82	63.04
	(9.9)	(6.1)	(5.2)	(5.3)	(5.0)	(5.3)	(5.9)	(5.5)
Thailand	7.12	23.07	57.20	54.49	58.50	68.96	65.11	68.85
	(3.8)	(5.5)	(6.5)	(5.9)	(6.0)	(5.9)	(5.9)	(5.8)
Malaysia	15.41	29.42	73.72	73.47	84.55	98.15	88.20	96.23
	(8.2)	(7.0)	(8.4)	(8.0)	(8.7)	(8.3)	(8.0)	(8.1)
Philippines	4.61	8.19	17.37	29.50	35.48	38.06	32.14	36.55
	(2.5)	(2.0)	(2.0)	(3.2)	(3.6)	(3.2)	(2.9)	(3.1)
Grand Total	187.08	419.04	877.39	916.91	975.87	1176.54	1100.67	1186.57

SOURCE: Asian Development Bank, *Key Indicators 2003*, www.adb.org.

TABLE 12: Total Exports to the United States ($US billion, with % shares of each exporting country in grand total)

COUNTRY	1985	1990	1995	1998	1999	2000	2001	2002
China	2.34	5.31	24.74	38.00	42.00	52.16	54.36	108.23
(PRC)	(4.6)	(5.6)	(14.3)	(19.2)	(19.6)	(20.8)	(24.2)	(41.5)
Hong Kong	9.30	19.82	37.85	40.70	41.50	47.08	42.41	17.93
	(18.2)	(21.0)	(21.9)	(20.5)	(19.3)	(18.8)	(18.9)	(6.9)
Taiwan	14.77	21.75	26.41	29.38	30.90	34.82	27.65	26.76
	(28.9)	(23.1)	(15.3)	(14.8)	(14.4)	(13.9)	(12.3)	(10.3)
Singapore	4.83	11.22	21.58	21.86	22.06	23.89	18.76	19.11
	(9.5)	(11.9)	(12.5)	(11.0)	(10.3)	(9.5)	(8.4)	(7.3)
South Korea	10.79	19.42	24.34	23.08	29.60	37.81	31.36	33.76
	(21.1)	(20.6)	(14.1)	(11.6)	(13.8)	(15.1)	(14.0)	(13.0)
Indonesia	4.04	3.36	6.32	7.05	6.91	8.49	9.92	9.44
	(7.9)	(3.6)	(3.7)	(3.6)	(3.2)	(3.4)	(4.4)	(3.6)
Thailand	1.40	5.24	10.08	12.18	12.67	14.71	13.25	13.52
	(2.7)	(5.6)	(5.8)	(6.1)	(5.9)	(5.9)	(5.9)	(5.2)
Malaysia	1.97	4.99	15.31	15.89	18.53	20.16	17.82	21.37
	(3.9)	(5.3)	(8.9)	(8.0)	(8.6)	(8.0)	(7.9)	(8.2)
Philippines	1.66	3.10	6.22	10.15	10.49	11.41	8.99	10.39
	(3.2)	(3.3)	(3.6)	(5.1)	(4.9)	(4.6)	(4.0)	(4.0)
Grand Total	51.10	94.21	172.85	198.26	214.66	250.52	224.51	260.51

SOURCE: Asian Development Bank, *Key Indicators 2003*, www.adb.org.

TABLE 13: Exports to the United States as a Percent of Total Exports

Country	1985	1990	1995	1998	1999	2000	2001	2002
China (PRC)	8.5	8.5	16.6	20.7	21.5	20.9	20.4	29.1
Hong Kong	30.8	24.1	21.8	23.4	23.9	23.3	22.3	12.9
Taiwan	48.1	32.4	23.6	26.6	25.4	23.5	22.5	20.5
Singapore	21.2	21.3	18.3	19.9	19.2	17.3	15.4	15.3
South Korea	35.6	28.6	18.5	17.4	20.6	22.0	20.9	22.0
Indonesia	21.7	13.1	13.9	14.4	14.2	13.7	15.3	14.5
Thailand	19.7	22.7	17.6	22.3	21.7	21.3	20.3	19.6
Malaysia	12.8	16.9	20.8	21.6	21.9	20.5	20.2	22.2
Philippines	35.9	37.9	35.8	34.4	29.6	30.0	28.0	28.4

SOURCE: Asian Development Bank, *Key Indicators 2003*, www.adb.org.

TABLE 14: Shares of Different Regional Markets in Exports
of East Asian Countries (by percent)

Exporting Country	Years	Asia	Western Europe	North and Central America	Rest of World
China (PRC)	1990	68.8	10.3	10.2	10.7
	1998	49.9	16.6	23.6	9.9
	2000	46.0	15.9	30.3	7.8
	2001	47.5	16.0	27.7	8.8
	2002	43.4	15.6	32.1	8.9
Hong Kong	1990	46.5	19.8	27.3	6.4
	1998	49.7	16.9	27.2	6.2
	2000	53.5	15.9	25.0	5.6
	2001	54.3	15.8	24.5	5.4
	2002	63.6	14.7	15.8	5.9
Taiwan	1990	38.2	18.2	36.0	7.6
	1998	51.2	13.9	34.9	0.0
	2000	56.4	12.7	30.9	0.0
	2001	56.4	12.7	30.9	0.0
	2002	56.9	14.2	23.0	5.9
Singapore	1990	51.1	15.9	23.1	9.9
	1998	51.0	18.3	22.5	8.2
	2000	57.2	15.4	20.4	7.0
	2001	58.6	15.2	18.4	7.8
	2002	61.8	13.0	17.3	7.9
South Korea	1990	35.4	15.5	33.4	15.7
	1998	41.3	19.9	22.9	15.9
	2000	43.0	16.2	29.3	11.5
	2001	44.7	15.1	27.1	13.1
	2002	46.1	13.2	27.9	12.8

TABLE 14 *continued*

Exporting Country	Years	Asia	Western Europe	North and Central America	Rest of World
Indonesia	1990	67.7	12.2	13.9	6.2
	1998	52.8	17.9	18.4	10.9
	2000	58.0	15.3	17.9	8.8
	2001	58.4	14.9	17.5	9.2
	2002	59.6	13.9	16.2	10.3
Thailand	1990	39.2	24.1	25.3	11.4
	1998	45.0	20.5	26.0	8.9
	2000	48.9	18.0	24.7	8.4
	2001	49.2	18.0	23.3	9.5
	2002	51.5	15.7	21.9	10.9
Malaysia	1990	59.8	15.6	18.1	6.5
	1998	50.8	17.7	24.2	7.3
	2000	53.8	14.9	24.9	6.4
	2001	55.6	14.9	22.7	6.8
	2002	56.3	13.0	23.7	7.0
Philippines	1990	37.5	18.8	40.2	3.5
	1998	37.1	21.9	38.6	2.4
	2000	42.1	19.7	35.9	2.3
	2001	46.6	18.2	32.8	2.4
	2002	48.6	17.4	30.7	3.3

SOURCE: Asian Development Bank, *Key Indicators 2000, Key Indicators 2001, Key Indicators 2002, Key Indicators 2003,* www.adb.org.

Notes

INTRODUCTION

1   The "Conference on the Work of Karl Marx and Challenges for the 21st Century" was held in Havana, Cuba, May 5–8, 2003. Papers can be found at www.nodo50.org/cubasigloXXI.

2   See, for example, William Hinton, *The Great Reversal: The Privatization of China, 1978–1989* (New York: Monthly Review Press, 1990); Maurice Meisner, *The Deng Xiaoping Era: An Inquiry into the Fate of Chinese Socialism, 1978–1994* (New York: Hill and Wang, 1996); Robert Weil, *Red Cat, White Cat: China and the Contradictions of "Market Socialism"* (New York: Monthly Review Press, 1996); Gerard Greenfield and Apo Leong, "China's Communist Capitalism: The Real World of Market Socialism," in Leo Panitch (ed.), *Socialist Register 1997: Ruthless Criticism of All That Exists* (New York: Monthly Review Press, 1997); Barbara Foley, "From Situational Dialectics to Pseudo-Dialectics: Mao, Jiang, and Capitalist Transition," *Cultural Logic* (2002), http://eserver.org/clogic/2002; Liu Yufan, "A Preliminary Report on China's Capitalist Restoration," *Links*, No. 21 (May–August 2002); Richard Smith "Creative Destruction: Capitalist Development and China's Environment," *New Left Review* 222 (March–April 1997); Eva Cheng, "China: Is Capitalist Restoration Inevitable?," *Links* 11 (January–April 1999). *See appendix for all tables referred to in text.

CHAPTER 1

1   UNCTAD, *World Investment Report 2002: Transnational Corporations and Export Competitiveness* (New York: United Nations, 2002).

2 Nicholas R. Lardy, "The Economic Rise of China: Threat or Opportunity?,"
   Economic Commentary, Federal Reserve Bank of Cleveland, August 1, 2003, p. 1.

3 Ronald I. McKinnon, *The Order of Economic Liberalization*, 2nd ed. (Baltimore:
   Johns Hopkins University Press, 1993).

4 Martin Hart-Landsberg, *The Rush to Development: Economic Growth and Political
   Struggle in South Korea* (New York: Monthly Review Press, 1993).

5 Paul Burkett and Martin Hart-Landsberg, *Development, Crisis and Class Struggle:
   Learning from Japan and East Asia* (New York: St. Martin's Press, 2000), chap. 13.

6 Martin Hart-Landsberg, "Challenging Neoliberal Myths: A Critical Look
   at the Mexican Experience," *Monthly Review* 54, no. 7 (December 2002).

7 Stephen Roach, "The Hypocrisy of Bashing China," *Financial Times*, August 7, 2003.

8 Shang-Jin Wei, "Is Globalization Good for the Poor in China?," *Finance
   and Development* 39, no. 3 (2002): 27.

9 Burkett and Hart-Landsberg, *Development, Crisis and Class Struggle*, chap. 11–12.

10 Eyal Press, "Rebel with a Cause: The Re-Education of Joseph Stiglitz,"
   The Nation, June 10, 2002, 13.

11 Joseph E. Stiglitz, *Globalization and Its Discontents* (New York: Norton, 2002), 125–26.

12 Press, "Rebel with a Cause: The Re-Education of Joseph Stiglitz," 13.

13 Ibid., 13–14.

14 Stiglitz, *Globalization and Its Discontents*, 184.

15 Vanessa Lau, "Forgotten Generation," *Dollars and Sense* (March–April 2000), 11.

16 Lardy, "The Economic Rise of China," 2.

17 M. J. Gordon, "China's Path to Market Socialism," *Challenge* 35, no. 1
   (January–February 1992): 53.

18 Victor D. Lippit, "But What About China?," *Rethinking Marxism* 6, no. 1
   (Spring 1993): 128–29.

19 John E. Roemer, "Can There by Socialism after Communism?," in *Market
   Socialism: The Current Debate*, ed. Pranab K. Bardhan and John E. Roemer (New
   York: Oxford University Press, 1993); John E. Roemer, *A Future for Socialism*
   (London: Verso, 1994); Paul Bowles and Xiao-yuan Dong, "Current Successes
   and Future Challenges in China's Economic Reforms," *New Left Review*,
   no. 208 (November–December 1994).

20 Julio Carranza, Luis Gutierrez, and Pedro Monreal, *Cuba: La Reconstruccion
   de la Economia* (preliminary draft) (Havana: Centro de Estudios sobre America,
   January 1995); Rolando H. Castaneda and George Plinio Montalvan, "The
   'New' Cuban Economic Model (Or Socialism With Cuban Characteristics),"

in *Cuba in Transition: Volume 5*, Fifth Annual Meeting of the Association
for the Study of the Cuban Economy, 1995.

21 Pedro Monreal, "Cuba: The Challenges of Being Global and Socialist...
    at the Same Time," *Socialism and Democracy* 15, no. 1 (Spring-Summer 2001): 16.

22 Ibid.

23 Maurice Meisner, *The Deng Xiaoping Era: An Inquiry Into the Fate of Chinese Socialism,
    1978–1994* (New York: Hill and Wang, 1996); Robert Weil, *Red Cat, White Cat: China
    and the Contradictions of "Market Socialism"* (New York: Monthly Review Press, 1996).

24 Karl Marx and Frederick Engels, *On Colonialism* (Moscow: Progress Publishers,
    1974); Karl Marx and Frederick Engels, *Marx and Engels on the United States* (Moscow:
    Progress Publishers, 1979); V. I. Lenin, *Imperialism, The Highest Stage of Capitalism*,
    in V. I. Lenin, *Selected Works*, vol. 5 (New York: International Publishers, 1943); Leon
    Trotsky, *The Permanent Revolution and Results and Prospects* (London: New Park, 1962).

25 Burkett and Hart-Landsberg, *Development, Crisis and Class Struggle*, chap. 4.

26 Constance Lever-Tracy, David Ip, and Noel Tracy, *The Chinese Diaspora and
    Mainland China: An Emerging Economic Synergy* (London: Macmillan, 1996);
    Constance Lever-Tracy and Noel Tracy, "The Three Faces of Capitalism and the
    Asian Crisis," *Bulletin of Concerned Asian Scholars* 31, no. 3 (July-September 1999).

27 Walden Bello, "China at 50: A View from the South," *Focus on the Global South*,
    1999, http://focusweb.org/popups/articleswindow.php?id=251.

28 Castaneda and Montalvan, "The 'New' Cuban Economic Model"; Roger R.
    Betancourt, "Cuba's Economic 'Reforms': Waiting for Fidel on the Eve of the
    Twenty-First Century," in *Cuba in Transition: Volume 9*, Ninth Annual Meeting
    of the Association for the Study of the Cuban Economy, 1999.

CHAPTER 2

1   Stephen Andors, *China's Industrial Revolution: Politics, Planning, and Management,
    1949 to the Present* (New York: Pantheon Books, 1977); John G. Gurley, *China's
    Economy and the Maoist Strategy* (New York: Monthly Review Press, 1976); E. L.
    Wheelwright and Bruce McFarlane, *The Chinese Road to Socialism, Economics
    of the Cultural Revolution* (New York: Monthly Review Press, 1970).

2   Craig R. Littler and Martin Lockett, "The Significance of Trade Unions in China,"
    Industrial Relations Journal 14, no. 4 (1983); Seung Wook Baek, "The Changing
    Trade Unions in China," *Journal of Contemporary Asia* 30, no. 1 (2000).

3   Jackie Sheehan, *Chinese Workers, A New History* (New York: Routledge Press, 1998).

4   Ibid., 69; Elizabeth J. Perry, "Shanghai's Strike Wave of 1957," *China Quarterly*, no. 137, as quoted by Sheehan, 69.

5   Tim Pringle, "Summary of the Chinese Labor Movement Since 1949," *China Labor Bulletin*, August 17, 2001.

6   Cliff DuRand, "The Exhaustion of Developmental Socialism: Lessons from China," *Monthly Review* 42, no. 7 (December 1990): 13.

7   Trini Leung Wing-yue, *Smashing the Iron Rice Pot: Workers and Unions in China's Market Socialism* (Hong Kong: Asia Monitor Resource Center, 1988), 3–4.

8   Maurice Meisner, *The Deng Xiaoping Era: An Inquiry Into the Fate of Chinese Socialism, 1978–1994* (New York: Hill and Wang, 1996), 189; Mobo C. F. Gao, "Debating the Cultural Revolution, Do We Only Know What We Believe?," *Critical Asian Studies* 34, no. 3 (September 2002): 424–25.

9   Meisner, *The Deng Xiaoping Era*, 192.

10 Eva Cheng, "China: Is Capitalist Restoration Inevitable?" *Links*, no. 11 (January–April 1999): 61.

11 Ibid., 60.

12 As quoted in Meisner, *The Deng Xiaoping Era*, 193.

13 DuRand, "The Exhaustion of Developmental Socialism," 11–3. There were also popular gains made during the Cultural Revolution. For example, there were important developments in medicine; farmers were trained as health care providers and new advances were made in using traditional medicine. Popular participation in cultural activities also grew, producing new developments in painting, music and theater. Similarly, there was also an explosion of magazines, newspapers, and books. "According to one estimate, for instance, more than ten thousand kinds of newspapers and pamphlets were published by the *laobaixing* [ordinary people] in China during the Cultural Revolution." See Mobo C. F. Gao, "Debating the Cultural Revolution, Do We Only Know What We Believe?," 428.

14 Malcolm Warner, "Industrial Relations in the Chinese Factory," *Journal of Industrial Relations*, 29, no. 2 (June 1987): 220.

15 Robert Weil, *Red Cat, White Cat: China and the Contradictions of "Market Socialism"* (New York: Monthly Review Press, 1996): 13.

16 Ibid., 230.

17 Leung Wing-yue, *Smashing the Iron Rice Pot*, 59–62.

18 Ibid., 61.

19 Cheng, "China: Is Capitalist Restoration Inevitable?" 53–4.

20 Meisner, *The Deng Xiaoping Era*, 265, 269.

21 Cheng, "China: Is Capitalist Restoration Inevitable?" 47.

22 Meisner, *The Deng Xiaoping Era*, 263.

23 Ibid., 221.

24 Cheng, "China: Is Capitalist Restoration Inevitable?" 61.

25   Ibid., 61.

26 Gerard Greenfield Apo Leong, "China's Communist Capitalism: The Real World
     of Market Socialism," in *Socialist Register 1997: Ruthless Criticism of All That Exists*,
     ed. Leo Panitch (New York: Monthly Review Press, 1997), 107.

27 Cheng, "China: Is Capitalist Restoration Inevitable?" 53.

28 Greenfield and Leong, "China's Communist Capitalism," 110.

29 Leung Wing-yue, *Smashing the Iron Rice Pot*, 65.

30 Greenfield and Leong, "China's Communist Capitalism," 112.

31 Cheng, "China: Is Capitalist Restoration Inevitable?" 52; Richard Smith,
     "Creative Destruction: Capitalist Development and China's Environment,"
     New Left Review, no. 222 (March–April 1997): 6, 10.

32 Smith, "Creative Destruction," 6; Anita Chan, *China's Workers Under Assault:
     The Exploitation of Labor in a Globalizing Economy* (Armonk, New York:
     M. E. Sharpe, 2001).

33 Meisner, *The Deng Xiaoping Era*, 235.

34 Ibid., 235.

35 Smith, "Creative Destruction," 10.

36 Meisner, *The Deng Xiaoping Era*, 238–9.

37 Cheng, "China: Is Capitalist Restoration Inevitable?" 50; Raymond Lau,
     "Economic Determination in the Last Instance: China's Political-Economic
     Development Under the Impact of the Asian Financial Crisis," *Historical
     Materialism*, no. 8 (Summer 2001): 221–22.

38 Meisner, *The Deng Xiaoping Era*, 289.

39 Cheng, "China: Is Capitalist Restoration Inevitable?" 54–5.

40 Liu Yufan, "A Preliminary Report on China's Capitalist Restoration," *Links*, no. 21
     (May–August 2002), 53.

41 Ching Kwan Lee, "From Organized Dependence to Disorganized Despotism:
     Changing Labor Regimes in Chinese Factories," *China Quarterly*, no. 157
     (March 1999), 55–56.

42 Leung Wing-yue, *Smashing the Iron Rice Pot*, 60.

43 Meisner, *The Deng Xiaoping Era*, 291.

44 Greenfield and Leong, "China's Communist Capitalism," 99.

45 Leung Wing-yue, *Smashing the Iron Rice Pot*, 61.

46 Ibid., 61.

47 John Child, "Changes in the Structure and Prediction of Earnings in Chinese
    State Enterprises During the Economic Reform," *International Journal
    of Human Resource Management* 6, no. 1 (February 1995); Warner, "Industrial
    Relations in the Chinese Factory," 226–28.

48 Leung Wing-yue, *Smashing the Iron Rice Pot*, 130–1.

49 Meisner, *The Deng Xiaoping Era*, 279.

50 Ibid., 373.

51 Asian Development Bank. *Key Indicators 2002*, www.adb.org, 128.

52 Meisner, *The Deng Xiaoping Era*, 294–5.

53 Weil, *Red Cat, White Cat*, 47.

54 Meisner, *The Deng Xiaoping Era*, 241.

55 Ibid., 386.

56 Leung Wing-yue, *Smashing the Iron Rice Pot*, 74.

57 Ibid., 74,

58 Cheng, "China: Is Capitalist Restoration Inevitable?" 50.

59 W. K. Lau, "The 15th Congress of the Chinese Communist Party: Milestone in
    China's Privatization," *Capital & Class*, no. 68 (Summer 1999): 52.

60 R. Lau, "Economic Determination in the Last Instance," 222.

61 Ibid., 222–3.

62 Cheng, "China: Is Capitalist Restoration Inevitable?" 45.

63 R. Lau, "Economic Determination in the Last Instance," 223.

64 UNCTAD, *Trade and Development Report 2002: Developing Countries in World Trade*
    (New York: United Nations, 2002), 148.

65 Russell Smyth, "Asset Stripping in Chinese State-Owned Enterprises,"
    Journal of Contemporary Asia 30, no. 1 (2000): 7.

66 R. Lau, "Economic Determination in the Last Instance," 246.

67 See, for example, Ben Fine, "Privatization: Theory and Lessons from the UK and
    South Africa," *Seoul Journal of Economics* 10, no. 4 (1997); Tony Killick and Simon
    Commander, "State Divestiture as a Policy Instrument in Developing Countries,"
    World Development 16, no. 12 (December 1988); T. T. Ram Mohan, "Privatization:
    Theory and Evidence," *Economic and Political Weekly*, December 29, 2001; Andong
    Zhu, "Growth, Equity and State Enterprises: International and Chinese
    Perspectives," paper presented at the *Rethinking Marxism* conference, "Marxism
    and the World Stage," Amherst, Massachusetts, November 6–8, 2003.

68 Carsten A. Holz, "Long Live China's State-Owned Enterprises: Deflating the
    Myth of Poor Financial Performance," *Journal of Asian Economics* 13, no. 4
    (July–August 2002).

69 Smith, "Creative Destruction," 12.

70 Smyth, "Asset Stripping in Chinese State-Owned Enterprises," 4–11.

71 Ibid., 3.

72 Ibid., 4.

73 Yufan, "A Preliminary Report on China's Capitalist Restoration," 54.

74 Cheng, "China: Is Capitalist Restoration Inevitable?" 45.

75 R. Lau, "Economic Determination in the Last Instance," 225.

76 W. K. Lau, "The 15th Congress of the Chinese Communist Party," 74.

77 Ibid., 33.

78 R. Lau, "Economic Determination in the Last Instance," 225.

79 Ibid., 226.

80 Ibid., 225.

81 Christopher Lingle, "China's Insoluble Banking Mess," *Taipei Times*, June 16, 2002.

82 Ronald I. McKinnon, *The Order of Economic Liberalization*, 2nd ed. (Baltimore:
    Johns Hopkins University Press, 1993), chap. 11.

83 R. Lau, "Economic Determination in the Last Instance," 224.

84 Samuel P. S. Ho, Paul Bowles, and Xiaoyuan Dong, "'Letting Go of the Small':
    An Analysis of the Privatization of Rural Enterprises in Jiangsu and Shandong,"
    Journal of Development Studies 39, no. 4 (2003): 8.

85 Ibid., 10.

86 Ibid., 19–21.

87 Elissa Braunstein and Gerald Epstein, "Bargaining Power and Foreign Direct
    Investment in China: Can 1.3 Billion Consumers Tame the Multinationals?,"
    Working Paper no. 46, Political Economy Research Institute, University
    of Massachusetts, Amherst (2002), 8.

88 Chen Zhilong, "Two Decades of Utilizing F D I in China: States, Structure and
    Impact," *China Report* 38, no. 4 (2002): 473.

89 Braunstein and Epstein, "Bargaining Power and Foreign Direct Investment
    in China," 7.

90 This was a rapid transformation, even by the standards of East Asian countries.
    For example, Malaysia's ratio of manufactured exports to total exports grew
    from 55.2 percent in 1990 to 76.8 percent in 1996. In Thailand, the percentage
    increased from 63.4 to 71.4 percent over the same period. See Dilip K. Das,

"Changing Comparative Advantage and the Changing Composition of Asian Exports," *World Economy* 21, no. 1 (1998): 125.

91   UNCTAD, *Trade and Development Report 2002*, 143.

92   Harry Magdoff, "A Note on 'Market Socialism'," *Monthly Review* 47, no. 1 (May 1985); Bertell Ollman, "Market Mystification in Capitalist and Market Socialist Societies," *Socialism and Democracy* 11, no. 2 (Fall 1997); Dimitris Milonakis, "New Market Socialism: A Case for Rejuvenation or Inspired Alchemy?" *Cambridge Journal of Economics* 27, no. 1 (January 2003).

93   Paul Burkett and Martin Hart-Landsberg, *Development, Crisis and Class Struggle: Learning from Japan and East Asia* (New York: St. Martin's Press, 2000).

CHAPTER 3

1   Paul Bowles and Gordon White, "Contradictions in China's Financial Reforms: The Relationship Between Banks and Enterprises," *Cambridge Journal of Economics* 13, no. 4 (December 1989): 485.

2   Ibid., 487.

3   Oktay Yenal, "Chinese Reforms, Inflation and the Allocation of Investment in a Socialist Economy," *World Development* 18, no. 5 (May 1990): 709.

4   Bowles and White, "Contradictions in China's Financial Reforms," 488.

5   W. K. Lau, "The 15th Congress of the Chinese Communist Party: Milestone in China's Privatization," *Capital & Class*, no. 68 (Summer 1999): 54.

6   Ibid., 78.

7   Cheng Yuk-shing, "Fleeing from the Asian Financial Crisis: China's Economic Policy in 1997–2000," *China Report* 38, no. 2 (2002): 265.

8   Ibid., 265.

9   Bowles and White, "Contradictions in China's Financial Reforms," 488.

10   Ibid., 485, 488.

11   John P. Bonin and Yiping Huang, "Dealing with the Bad Loans of the Chinese Banks," *Journal of Asian Economics* 12, no. 2 (Summer 2001): 198.

12   Ibid., 199–200.

13   Keith Bradsher, "Another Asian Nation Battling a Crisis In Its Banking System," *New York Times*, October 26, 2002; David Lague, "A Government Move to Clean Up Loans Backfires," *Far Eastern Economic Review*, November 14, 2002.

14   Christopher Lingle, "China's Economic Data Still Erratic," *Taipei Times*, March 10, 2002.

15   Andong Zhu, "Growth, Equity and State Enterprises: International and Chinese

Perspectives," paper presented at the *Rethinking Marxism* Conference, "Marxism and the World Stage," Amherst, Massachusetts, November 6–8, 2003, 35.

16   IHLO (International Hong Kong Liaison Office), "Official Jobless Rate in China," *Monthly News Bulletin*, November 18, 2002, http://www.ihlo.org/item1/item1u.htm.

17   Ching Kwan Lee, "From Organized Dependence to Disorganized Despotism: Changing Labor Regimes in Chinese Factories," *China Quarterly*, no. 157 (March 1999): 55–56.

18   Raymond Lau, "Economic Determination in the Last Instance: China's Political-Economic Development Under the Impact of the Asian Financial Crisis," *Historical Materialism*, no. 8 (Summer 2001): 233.

19   Eva Cheng, "China: Is Capitalist Restoration Inevitable?," *Links*, no. 11 (January–April 1999), 62–63.

20   Rene Ofreneo, "Changing Labor Markets in a Globalizing Asia: Challenges for Trade Unions," *Asian Labor Update*, no. 45 (October–December 2002); Richard Smith, "Creative Destruction: Capitalist Development and China's Environment," *New Left Review*, no. 222 (March–April 1997): 6.

21   R. Smith, "Creative Destruction," 6.

22   "China Admits Grim Unemployment Situation," *Times of India*, April 29, 2002.

23   Gene H. Chang, "The Cause and Cure of China's Widening Income Disparity," *China Economic Review* 13, no. 4 (2002): 337.

24   Liu Yufan, "A Preliminary Report on China's Capitalist Restoration," *Links*, no. 21 (May–August 2002): 55.

25   Keith Bradsher, "China's Car Culture Hits Some Potholes," *New York Times*, January 11, 2004; Craig S. Smith, "For China's Wealthy, All But Fruited Plain," *New York Times*, May 15, 2002; Elisabeth Rosenthal, "North of Beijing, California Dreams Come True," *New York Times*, February 3, 2003.

26   Craig S. Smith, "China: Heroes of Capitalism," *New York Times*, May 2, 2002.

27   Malcolm Warner, "In the Red: China's State-owned Enterprises at the Crossroads," *Asia Pacific Business Review* 5, no. 2 (Winter 1998): 224; Vanessa Lau, "Forgotten Generation," *Dollars and Sense* (March–April 2000): 12.

28   V. Lau, "Forgotten Generation," 12.

29   Margaret Maurer-Fazio and James Hughes, "The Effects of Market Liberalization on the Relative Earnings of Chinese Women," *Journal of Comparative Economics* 30, no. 4 (December 2002).

30   Joseph Kahn, "Ruse in Toyland: Chinese Workers' Hidden Woe," *New York Times*, December 7, 2003; Smith, "Creative Destruction," 7–9; Philip P. Pan, "Poisoned

Back into Poverty," *Washington Post*, August 4, 2002.

31 Elisabeth Rosenthal, "Harsh Chinese Reality Feeds a Black Market in Women," *New York Times*, June 25, 2001; Erik Eckholm, "Desire for Sons Drives Use of Prenatal Scan in China," *New York Times*, June 21, 2002.

32 Tim Pringle, "The Path of Globalization: Implications for Chinese Workers," *Asian Labor Update*, no. 41 (October–December 2001).

33 Joseph Kahn, "Making Trinkets in China, and a Deadly Dust," *New York Times*, June 18, 2003.

34 Joseph Kahn, "China's Workers Risk Limbs in Export Drive," *New York Times*, April 7, 2003.

35 Lau, "Economic Determination in the Last Instance," 234.

36 Smith, "Creative Destruction," 10–11.

37 Pan, "Poisoned Back into Poverty."

38 Elisabeth Rosenthal, "Without 'Barefoot Doctors,' China's Rural Families Suffer," *New York Times*, March 14, 2001, A1.

39 Cheng, "China: Is Capitalist Restoration Inevitable?," 61.

40 Ibid., 61.

41 Elisabeth Rosenthal, "Blinded by Poverty: The Dark Side of Capitalism," *New York Times*, November 21, 2000, .

42 Ibid.

43 V. Lau, "Forgotten Generation," 13–14; Pan, "Poisoned Back into Poverty."

44 David Murphy, "The SARS Outbreak: A Shot in the Arm," *Far Eastern Economic Review*, June 5, 2003.

45 Jiang Xueqin, "Consuming Problem," *Far Eastern Economic Review*, December 21, 2000; Elisabeth Rosenthal, "Deadly Shadow Darkens Remote Chinese Village," *New York Times*, May 28, 2001.

46 Isabel Hilton, "Economic Liberalization Destroyed China's Health Service—Now It Must Rely on Police, Not Doctors, to Fight Sars," *Guardian*, May 22, 2003.

47 V. Lau, "Forgotten Generation," 39.

48 Ben Dolven and Trish Saywell, "Private Lessons," *Far Eastern Economic Review*, January 8, 2004.

49 Elisabeth Rosenthal, "School a Rare Luxury for Rural Chinese Girls," *New York Times*, November 1, 1999.

50 Ibid.

51 Ibid.

52 Lee, "From Organized Dependence to Disorganized Despotism," 54.

53 "A Dragon Out of Puff," *The Economist*, June 13, 2002.

54 Kathy Wilhelm, "The Great Divide," *Far Eastern Economic Review*, November 30, 2000.

55 Cheng Yuk-shing, "Fleeing from the Asian Financial Crisis," 267.

56 Bertell Ollman, "The Question Is Not 'When Will Capitalism Die?' but 'When Did It Die, and What Should Our Reaction Be?'," *Nature, Society, and Thought* 12, no. 4 (October 1999), 474–475.

57 Ibid., 475.

58 Yufan, "A Preliminary Report on China's Capitalist Restoration," 55.

59 Cheng Yuk-shing, "Fleeing from the Asian Financial Crisis," 269.

60 Ibid., 271.

61 Ibid.

62 Bonin and Huang, "Dealing with the Bad Loans of the Chinese Banks," 201.

63 Cheng Yuk-shing, "Fleeing from the Asian Financial Crisis," 272.

64 Ben Dolven, "The Danger of Blowing Bubbles," *Far Eastern Economic Review*, September 25, 2003, 33.

65 Ibid.

66 *Wall Street Journal*, "China Warns Exporters to Shape Up," March 18, 1999; Kathy Wilhelm, "China, Starting to Sizzle," *Far Eastern Economic Review*, August 24, 2000.

67 Stephen Roach, "China's Economy—It's the Real Thing," *South China Morning Post*, February 26, 2003.

68 Eva Cheng, "China: Sino-U.S. Trade Deal Will Cement Capitalist Restoration," *Green Left Weekly*, no. 406, May 24, 2000.

69 Yufan, "A Preliminary Report on China's Capitalist Restoration," 56.

70 Ibid., 57.

71 Ibid..

72 Ofreneo, "Changing Labor Markets in a Globalizing Asia."

73 Elizabeth Tang, "China and the WTO: A Trade Union View of Social Impacts & Workers' Responses," Hong Kong Confederation of Trade Unions, May 2002, http://www.ihlo.org/item3/item3h.htm.

74 UNCTAD, *Trade and Development Report 2002: Developing Countries in World Trade* (New York: United Nations, 2002), 143.

75 Ibid., 149.

76 Yufan, "A Preliminary Report on China's Capitalist Restoration," 58.

77 Jackie Sheehan, *Chinese Workers, A New History* (New York: Routledge Press, 1998), 187.

78 Ibid., 187–88.

79 Trini Leung, "The Third Wave of the Chinese Labor Movement in the Post-Mao

Era," *China Labor Bulletin*, June 2, 2002.

80 Trini Leung Wing-yue, *Smashing the Iron Rice Pot: Workers and Unions in China's Market Socialism* (Hong Kong: Asia Monitor Resource Center, 1988); Anita Chan, "Labor's Long March: China's Workers Rebel Against the New World Order," *In These Times*, February 6, 1995.

81 R. Smith, "Creative Destruction," 9.

82 Eric Eckholm, "Chinese Democracy Campaigners Push for Free Labor Unions," *New York Times*, December 24, 1997.

83 Associated Press, "China's New Threat: Army of Unemployment Creating Wave of Protests Across Nation," *Tribune-Star*, Terre Haute, December 26, 1997.

84 Henry Chu, "Chinese Rulers Fear Angry Workers May Finally Unite," *Los Angeles Times*, June 4, 1999.

85 Tim Pringle, "Industrial Unrest in China—A Labor Movement in the Making?," *China Labor Bulletin*, January 31, 2002.

86 Ibid.

87 Leung, "The Third Wave."

88 Tang, "China and the WTO."

89 Leung, "The Third Wave."

90 Ibid.

91 Chu, "Chinese Rulers Fear Angry Workers May Finally Unite."

92 Craig S. Smith, "China's Farmers Rebel Against Bureaucracy," *New York Times*, September 17, 2000, 1.

93 Ibid.

94 "Troubled Sleep in Sichuan," *The Economist*, July 26, 1997, 35.

95 Ibid.

96 Associated Press, "China's New Threat."

97 Leung, "The Third Wave."

98 Sophie Beach, "Tiananmen Plus Ten," *The Nation*, June 14, 1999, 7.

99 Erik Eckholm, "China: Crowd Control," *New York Times*, November 25, 1999.

100 Chu, "Chinese Rulers Fear Angry Workers May Finally Unite."

101 Erik Eckholm, "Chinese Officials Order Cities To Bolster Riot Police Forces," *New York Times*, January 30, 2001.

102 Dong Xulin, "Looming Social Crises: China at a Cross Road," paper presented at the *Socialist Scholars Conference*, New York, March 16, 2003.

CHAPTER 4

1   Stephen Roach, "China's Economy—It's the Real Thing," *South China Morning Post*, February 26, 2003, 19.

2   Bank for International Settlements, *73rd Annual Report* (Basel, Switzerland: Bank for International Settlements, 2003), 44.

3   Elena Ianchovichina, Sethaput Suthiwart-Narueput, and Min Zhao, "Regional Impact of China's WTO Accession," in *East Asia Integrates: A Trade Policy Agenda for Shared Growth*, ed. Kathie Krumm and Homi Kharas (Washington D.C.: World Bank, 2003), 57.

4   UNCTAD, *World Investment Report 2002: Transnational Corporations and Export Competitiveness* (New York: United Nations, 2002), 161.

5   Mi-Kyung Jung, "China, Emerging Giant in Electronics Market," *Dong-A Ilbo*, May 4, 2003.

6   Stephen Roach, "The Hypocrisy of Bashing China," *Financial Times*, August 7, 2003.

7   UNCTAD, *World Investment Report 2001: Promoting Linkages* (New York: United Nations, 2001), 26.

8   Rene Ofreneo, "Changing Labor Markets in a Globalizing Asia: Challenges for Trade Unions," *Asian Labor Update*, no. 45 (October–December 2002).

9   Bank for International Settlements, 44–5.

10 UNCTAD, *Trade and Development Report 2002: Developing Countries in World Trade* (New York: United Nations, 2002), 156.

11 Ramkishen Rajan, "Emergence of China as an Economic Power: What Does It Imply for South-East Asia?" *Economic and Political Weekly*, June 28, 2003, 2639–40.

12 David Roland-Holst, "An Overview of PRC's Emergence and East Asian Trade Patterns to 2020," Research Paper no. 44, *Asian Development Bank Institute* (October 2002), 6.

13 Ibid., 8.

14 Suthiphand Chirathivat, "ASEAN-China Free Trade Area: Background, Implications and Future Development," *Journal of Asian Economics* 13, no. 5 (September–October 2002), 674.

15 Thitapha Wattanapruttipaisan, "ASEAN-China Free Trade Area: Advantages, Challenges, and Implications for the Newer ASEAN Member Countries," *ASEAN Economic Bulletin* 20, no. 1 (April 2003), 45.

16 Martin Hart-Landsberg, *The Rush to Development: Economic Growth and Political Struggle in South Korea* (New York: Monthly Review Press, 1993); Paul Burkett

and Martin Hart-Landsberg, "Contradictions of Capitalist Industrialization in East Asia: A Critique of 'Flying Geese' Theories of Development," *Economic Geography* 74, no. 2 (April 1998); Paul Burkett and Martin Hart-Landsberg, *Development, Crisis and Class Struggle: Learning from Japan and East Asia* (New York: St. Martin's Press, 2000); Paul Burkett and Martin Hart-Landsberg, "A Critique of 'Catch-Up' Theories of Development," *Journal of Contemporary Asia* 33, no. 2 (2003); Paul Burkett and Martin Hart-Landsberg, "The Economic Crisis in Japan: Mainstream Perspectives and an Alternative View," *Critical Asian Studies* 35, no. 3 (September 2003).

17 Paul Burkett and Martin Hart-Landsberg, "Crisis and Recovery in East Asia: The Limits of Capitalist Development," *Historical Materialism*, no. 8 (Summer 2001).

18 Eva Cheng, "China: Is Capitalist Restoration Inevitable?," *Links*, no. 11 (January–April 1999); Raymond Lau, "Economic Determination in the Last Instance: China's Political-Economic Development Under the Impact of the Asian Financial Crisis," *Historical Materialism*, no. 8 (Summer 2001); Liu Yufan, "A Preliminary Report on China's Capitalist Restoration," *Links*, no. 21 (May–August 2002).

19 Fred Herschede, "Competition Among ASEAN, China, and the East Asian NICs: A Shift-Share Analysis," ASEAN *Economic Bulletin* 7, no. 3 (March 1991); Jan P. Voon and Ren Yue, "China-ASEAN Export Rivalry in the U.S. Market: The Importance of the HK-China Production Synergy and the Asian Financial Crisis," *Journal of the Asia Pacific Economy* 8, no. 2 (2003); Nicholas R. Lardy, "The Economic Rise of China: Threat or Opportunity?," *Economic Commentary*, Federal Reserve Bank of Cleveland, August 1, 2003, 3.

20 *Japan Times*, "China Seen as 'Second Engine' of Growth for ASEAN Nations," April 25, 2003.

21 Ianchovichina et al., "Regional Impact of China's WTO Accession," 66.

22 Ibid., 67.

23 Tham Siew-Yean, "Can Malaysian Manufacturing Compete with China in the WTO?," *Asia-Pacific Development Journal* 8, no. 2 (December 2001), 11.

24 Ianchovichina et al., "Regional Impact of China's WTO Accession," 69–70.

25 John McBeth, "Warning Signs," *Far Eastern Economic Review*, December 4, 2003.

26 Ibid.

27 Ianchovichina et al., "Regional Impact of China's WTO Accession," 72–73.

28 Tham, "Can Malaysian Manufacturing Compete," 5.

29 Erik Eckholm and Joseph Kahn, "Asia Worries About Growth of China's Economic Power," *New York Times*, November 24, 2002, 6.

30 Leslie Lopez, "Hidden Weakness," *Far Eastern Economic Review*, November 20, 2003.

31 Tham, "Can Malaysian Manufacturing Compete," 12.

32 Karby Leggett and Peter Wonacott, "Burying the Competition," *Far Eastern Economic Review*, October 17, 2002.

33 Elgin Toh, "China Hits Singapore Hardest in Asean," *Business Times* (Singapore), February 11, 2003.

34 Barry Wain, "Identity Crisis," *Far Eastern Economic Review*, September 4, 2003, 19.

35 Rajan, "Emergence of China as an Economic Power," 2643.

36 Alan Wheatley, "Asia Seeks Answer to China's Ascent," *Reuters News Service*, March 9, 2003.

37 John Wong and Sarah Chan, "China's Emergence as a Global Manufacturing Center: Implications for ASEAN," *Asia Pacific Business Review* 9, no. 1 (Autumn 2002), 91.

38 Wheatley, "Asia Seeks Answer."

39 Kim Mi-hui, "Korea Outpaces Japan, Taiwan in China," *Korea Herald*, June 4, 2003.

40 Ibid.

41 William Pesek Jr., "South Korea's Roh Looks to China, Not Japan," *Bloomberg.com*, May 20, 2003.

42 Andrew Ward, "South Korea Feels the Chill in China's Shadow," *Financial Times*, September 25, 2003.

43 We discuss South Korea's post-crisis restructuring in more detail in Martin Hart-Landsberg and Paul Burkett, "Economic Crisis and Restructuring in South Korea: Beyond the Free Market-Statist Debate," *Critical Asian Studies* 33, no. 3 (September 2001).

44 Yoo Cheong-mo, "Seoul Hopes Cash Will Lure Foreign Firms," *Korea Herald*, June 6, 2003.

45 Kim Hyun-chul, "Chaebol Lobby Warns of Exodus," *Korea Herald*, June 27, 2003.

46 Moon Ihlwan, "South Korea: Can Roh Handle a Summer of Strikes?," *Business Week*, July 7, 2003, 46.

47 Don Kirk, "Contract at Hyundai Raises Sights of Korean Workers," *New York Times*, August 19, 2003, W1, W7.

48 Lee Joo-hee, "More Home Electronics Plants Move Overseas," *Korea Herald*, January 9, 2003.

49 Ward, "South Korea Feels the Chill."

50 Caroline G. Cooper, "China and Korea: Partners or Competitors?," *Korea Insight*, 4, no. 9 (September 2000), 1.

51 Caroline G. Cooper, "Trade Winds Blow from West to East," in *Korea's Economy 2003*, ed. Korea Economic Institute (Washington, D.C.: Korea Economic Institute, 2003), 54.

52 Caroline Cooper, "Does China Pose an Economic Threat to Korea?," *Korea Insight* 4, no. 1 (January 2002), 1.

53 Cooper, "Trade Winds Blow from West to East," 55–56.

54 Ianchovichina et al., "Regional Impact of China's WTO Accession," 63.

55 Anthony Rowley, "China Beats U.S. to Emerge as Top Exporter to Japan," *Business Times*, February 19, 2003.

56 James Brooke, "Japan's Recovering Economy is Relying Heavily on China," *New York Times*, November 21, 2003.

57 Ronald Morse, "Long March Back to China," *Japan Times*, May 17, 2003.

58 Brooke, "Japan's Recovering Economy Is Relying Heavily on China."

59 Henry Sender, "A Rude Awakening," *Far Eastern Economic Review*, November 13, 2003.

60 Ibid.

61 Morse, "Long March Back to China."

62 Suvendrini Kakuchi, "Japan Strives to Adapt to a Strong China," *Asia Times* Taiwan), April 2, 2003.

63 Burkett and Hart-Landsberg, "Contradictions of Capitalist Industrialization in East Asia," 92–97; Burkett and Hart-Landsberg, *Development, Crisis and Class Struggle*, 116–20.

64 Burkett and Hart-Landsberg, "The Economic Crisis in Japan," 351.

65 James Brooke, "Hot Growth in China Brings Chill to Japan," *New York Times*, November 22, 2001.

66 Morse, "Long March Back to China."

67 Ianchovichina, et al., "Regional Impact of China's WTO Accession," 64.

68 James Brooke, "Accelerating Decline in Japan Evokes Rust Belt Comparisons," *New York Times*, August 31, 2001.

69 Surprisingly, some non-neoliberal economists see the shift of Japanese production to China as another step in the successful regionalization of the Japanese development model. See, for example, Edith Terry, "Crisis? What Crisis?," Working Paper no. 50, Japan Policy Research Institute, October 1998; and Edith Terry, "The World Bank and Japan," Working Paper no. 70, Japan Policy Research Institute, August 2000. We have dealt with this view elsewhere in Burkett and Hart-Landsberg, "Contradictions of Capitalist Industrialization in East Asia"; and Burkett and Hart-Landsberg, "The Economic Crisis in Japan."

70 Geri Smith, "Mexico, Wasting Away," *Business Week*, June 2, 2003, 42.

71 Ibid., 44.

72 Juan Forero, "As China Gallops, Mexico Sees Factory Jobs Slip Away," *New York Times*, September 3, 2003.

73 Smith, "Mexico, Wasting Away," 44.

74 Forero, "As China Gallops, Mexico Sees Factory Jobs Slip Away," A3.

75 Martin Hart-Landsberg, "Challenging Neoliberal Myths: A Critical Look at the Mexican Experience," *Monthly Review* 54, no. 7 (December 2002).

76 Ron Scherer, "Booming China Trade Rankles U.S.," *Christian Science Monitor*, August 5, 2003.

77 Leggett and Wonacott, "Burying the Competition."

78 James Burke, "U.S. Investment in China Worsens Trade Deficit," Briefing Paper, Economic Policy Institute, 2001, 2.

79 Scherer, "Booming China Trade Rankles U.S."

80 Richard McGregor, "Thriving U.S. Companies Ignore China Trade Surplus Issue," *Financial Times*, August 7, 2003.

81 Burke, "U.S. Investment in China Worsens Trade Deficit," 4.

82 Anwar M. Shaikh, Gennaro Zezza and Claudio H. Dos Santos, "Is International Growth the Way Out of U.S. Current Account Deficits? A Note of Caution," Policy Note 2003/6, Jerome Levy Economics Institute, 2003.

83 G. Pierre Goad, "Economies: Turning Point," *Far Eastern Economic Review*, August 31, 2000.

84 Gene H. Chang, "The Cause and Cure of China's Widening Income Disparity," *China Economic Review* 13, no. 4 (2002), 337; Yufan, "A Preliminary Report on China's Capitalist Restoration," 55.

85 Keith Bradsher, "Consumerism Grows in China, With Beijing's Blessing," *New York Times*, December 1, 2003.

86 Thomas Crampton, "China's Bounding Economy Fuels Both Hope and Concern," *New York Times*, November 11, 2003; Ben Dolven, "The Danger of Blowing Bubbles," *Far Eastern Economic Review*, September 25, 2003.

87 Asian Development Bank, *Key Indicators 2002*, www.adb.org, 124–25; Asian Development Bank, *Key Indicators 2003*, www.adb.org, 157.

88 Edmund L. Andrews, "Imports Don't Deserve All That Blame," *New York Times*, December 7, 2003, 4.

89 Karl Marx, *Wage-Labor and Capital* (New York: International Publishers, 1976), 45.

CHAPTER 5

1   Robert Weil, "On 'Emancipating the Mind'," *Socialism and Democracy* 15, no. 2 (Fall 2001); Barbara Foley, "From Situational Dialectics to Pseudo-Dialectics: Mao, Jiang, and Capitalist Transition," *Cultural Logic*, 2002, http://eserver.org/clogic/2002.

2   Marx writing to the editorial board of *Otechestvenniye Zapiski*, November 1877, in Karl Marx and Frederick Engels, *Selected Correspondence* (Moscow: Progress Publishers, 1975), 294.

3   David McNally, "Language, History, and Class Struggle," *Monthly Review* 47, no. 3 (July/August 1995): 26–27.

4   Ibid., 26.

5   Clive Y. Thomas, *Dependence and Transformation: The Economics of the Transition to Socialism* (New York: Monthly Review Press, 1974).

6   See, for example, Sergio Diaz-Briquets, *The Health Revolution in Cuba* (Austin: University of Texas Press, 1983); Julie Margot Feinsilver, *Healing the Masses: Cuban Health Politics at Home and Abroad* (Berkeley: University of California Press, 1993); Kamran Nayeri, "The Cuban Health Care System and Factors Currently Undermining It," *Journal of Community Health* 20, no. 4 (August 1995); Amina Aitsiselme, "Despite U.S. Embargo, Cuban Biotech Booms," *NACLA Report on the Americas*, 35, no. 5 (March–April 2002); Mark Ingebretsen, "A Biotechnology Powerhouse Is Emerging Off Our Shores," The Daily Scan (*Wall Street Journal* website), November 25, 2003; Ernesto López Mola, Boris E. Acevedo, Ricardo Silva, Bianca Tormo, Ricardo Montero, and Luis Herrera, "Development of Cuban Biotechnology," *Journal of Commercial Biotechnology* 9, no. 2 (January 2003); *Reuters*, "Cuban Vaccine to Help Poor Kids," November 23, 2003.

7   Paul Burkett and Martin Hart-Landsberg, *Development, Crisis and Class Struggle: Learning from Japan and East Asia* (New York: St. Martin's Press, 2000), Chapters 11–12.

Index

agriculture, 37-38, 43-46, 50
All-China Federation of Trade Unions, 35
Association of Southeast Asian Nations
    (ASEAN), 91, 101, 118
ASEAN Free Trade Area (AFTA), 92
ASEAN-China Free Trade Area (ACFTA),
    92-93, 100
Asian Crisis of 1997-98, 18, 22-23, 29, 94
Asset Management Companies
    (AMCs), 65, 74
autonomous worker federations
    (WAFs), 80-81

Bank for International Settlements, 90
banks
    in China, 55-57, 63-64, 73
Beach, Sophie, 85
Beijing Autonomous Workers'
    Federation, 80
Bello, Walden, 30-31
Bowles, Paul, 57
Braunstein, Elissa, 59
Bullinger, Hans-Jorg, 111
bureaucracy, 9

capitalism, 7, 116
    restoration, 12, 18, 65
Castro, Fidel, 17, 27
central planning, 35, 38, 42
    weakening, 16, 46-47
Cheng, Eva, 55, 75-6
Chia Siow Yue, 95
Chiang Kai-Shek, 15
Chiang Kwan Lee, 66, 71
Chirathivat, Suthiphand, 93
class struggle, 9, 19, 43, 79-85, 116-118
communes, 43-46
Communist Party of China, 15-16, 34,
    39-40, 46, 49, 52-54, 58, 85, 111, 115
confusion about China, 18, 31-33
consumption
    versus investment, 10-11
    exploitation as limit on, 72, 112
Cuba, 17, 27-28, 119
Cultural Revolution, 35, 37-39, 79,
    137n.13

Daewoo Electronics, 103
Daqing Provisional Union of Retrenched

Workers, 83, 85
deflation, 73
Democracy Wall Movement (1978-81), 79
Deng Xiaoping, 36-37, 39, 42, 51, 62-63, 79-80

ecological crisis, 11-12, 94, 116
Economy, Elizabeth, 11
education, 38, 71
Epstein, Gerald, 59
export-led growth, 78, 94, 108-112, 114-115
China, 18-20, 59-61, 75, 87-91

Federation of Korean Industries, 103
Falun Gong, 85
Foreign Direct Investment (FDI), 24, 30-31, 112-115, 118
by Chinese firms, 11
in China, 20-21, 42, 48-49, 59-61, 75, 78, 88-91
in Cuba, 17, 27
in Southeast Asia, 22, 88-101
in South Korea, 88, 101-105
Free Trade Unions of China, 81

Gini coefficient, 67
Goad, Pierre, 111
Gordon, M.J., 26
Greater China, 30
Great Leap Forward, 35
Greenfield, Gerard, 48
growth, 9, 37, 50, 64, 87

health care, 38, 69-71, 119
Hired-Hand Workers Federation, 81
HIV, 70
Ho, Samuel P.S., 57
Hong Kong, 91
housing, 38, 69

imperialism, 76
India, 67
Indonesia, 67, 91, 95-97
inequality, 8-11, 38, 67, 72, 111
inflation, 42-43, 49-51, 64
interest rates, 73
International Monetary Fund (IMF), 21, 118
investment, 10-11

Japan, 93, 101, 105-108
as development model, 29
shift of production to China, 98-99, 106-108, 148n.69
Japan Electronic and Information Technology Industries Association, 89

Korea Economic Institute, 104
Korea Trade-Investment Promotion Agency, 101
Korean International Trade Association, 104

labor contracting, 41, 47-48
Lardy, Nicholas, 25
Lau, W.K., 52
League for the Protection of Rights of Working People, 81
Lenin, V.I., 32
Leong, Apo, 48
Leung, Trini, 83
LG Electronics, 103
Lian, Daniel, 100-101
Lippit, Victor, 26
Liu Yufan, 73, 78

Malaysia, 29, 91, 95, 97-99
Mao Zedong, 7, 15, 35, 62, 67
manufactured exports
China, 88-91, 95-101

Southeast Asia, 90-92, 95-101, 140n.90
South Korea, 101-105
maquiladora, 109
market socialism, 8, 10, 13, 26-27, 34, 39-40, 52
Marx, Karl, 32, 55, 113
Marxism, 17-18, 28, 33, 115-116, 120
May Day, 67
Matsushita Electric Works, Ltd., 107
Meisner, Maurice, 37, 45
Mexico, 23, 108-109
Mitsubishi Corporation, 109

neoliberalism
    China, 21-25, 32-33
    China's neighbors, 91-94
Normal Trade Relations (NTR)
    agreement, 75-76

Ofreneo, Rene, 66, 76, 90
Ollman, Bertell, 72
Opium War, 15
overproduction, 72, 74-75, 88, 94, 111-112

Pan Yue, 111
pensions, 69, 74
People's Bank of China, 64-65
Philippines, 96
postmodernism, 28
Pringle, Tim, 68, 82
privatization, 52-55, 57

Rajan, Ramkishen, 92
Roach, Stephen, 75, 87, 89
Roland-Holst, David, 92
rural development, 38, 43-46, 50

Sachs, Jeffrey, 21
Samsung Electronics, 103
SARS, 70-71

Selden, Mark, 38
Sheehan, Jackie, 35
shock therapy, 21, 25
Singapore, 91, 95
Smyth, Russell, 55
Social and Economic Policy Institute, 66
socialism, 86, 114
    development, 117-120
    transition, 7-8
socialist market economy, 16
South Korea, 29, 91, 101-105, 118
Soviet Union, 21, 25
speculation, 74-75
state budget, 55-57, 65, 73-74
state-owned enterprises (SOEs), 46-47, 52-57, 60
    debts, 55-57, 63-65
    worker layoffs, 65-66
Stiglitz, Joseph, 22-25, 30
strikes, 35, 47, 79, 81-82
students, 80

Taiwan, 91, 101
taxation, 56, 64
Thailand, 29, 67, 91, 95, 97
There Is No Alternative (TINA), 22
Tiananmen Incident of 1976, 36
Toh Kin Woon, 100
tourism, 100-101
Township and Village Enterprises (TVEs), 44-45, 49, 51, 57-58
Trotsky, Leon, 32

unemployment, 43, 65-67, 73, 113
uneven development, 19, 28, 88, 114
unions, 35, 39, 80-81
United Nations Conference on Trade and Development (UNCTAD), 60, 77
United States, 108-110, 113
Urban Collective Enterprises, 41-42

Vietnam, 27

wages, 38, 43, 45, 72-73, 111
Wang Dongjin, 67
Washington Consensus, 24
Weil, Robert, 39-40
World Bank, 21, 95-97, 108
World Trade Organization (WTO), 60,
    75-78, 90, 96, 104-107
women workers, 67-68, 71, 81, 116
work conditions, 68-69
Wu Yi, 11

Xianglong Dai, 57, 66
Xiaoyuan Dong, 57

Zhao Ziyang, 49
Zhou Enlai, 36